QUEENSLAND TRAVEL GUIDE 2023

A Comprehensive Travel Guide for 2023 and Beyond

Silva Martin

DISCLAIMER

The information in this "QUEENSLAND TRAVEL
GUIDE 2023: A Comprehensive Travel Guide for
2023 and Beyond" is provided for general
informational purposes only. While we strive for
accuracy, we make no warranties regarding the
completeness, accuracy, reliability, or suitability
of the information. The use of this guide is at your
own risk. We are not liable for any loss or damage
incurred. Links to external websites are provided
for convenience, and we have no control over
their content. The guide may experience
temporary unavailability due to technical issues
beyond our control. Travel conditions can change,
so verify information with relevant authorities.
All rights reserved. No reproduction or
transmission without written permission.

TABLE OF CONTENTS

EXPLORE

QUEENSLAND

WELCOME TO QUEENSLAND

In the summer of 2023, James embarked on a thrilling journey to explore the wonders of Queensland, Australia. His adventure began in the vibrant city of Brisbane, where he marvelled at the modern skyline that blended harmoniously with historic architecture. Wandering through the Queensland Cultural Centre, James immersed himself in the rich arts and cultural heritage of the region, absorbing the vibrant energy that permeated the city's streets.

Leaving the urban landscape behind, James set off to discover the natural wonders of Queensland. He snorkelling in the Great Barrier Reef, mesmerised by the kaleidoscope of colours beneath the crystal-clear waters. Swimming alongside vibrant coral formations and exotic marine life, he felt like a part of this thriving underwater paradise.

Continuing his journey, James ventured into the ancient Daintree Rainforest. The dense canopy enveloped him as he hiked through winding trails, captivated by the chorus of exotic birds and the symphony of nature. The towering trees and rare *flora left him in awe, fostering a deep connection with the untouched beauty of the wilderness.*

The allure of the Outback beckoned, and James embarked on an epic road trip. As he traversed the vast red landscapes, he encountered remote towns and experienced the unique lifestyle of the outback communities. James found himself immersed in the ruggedness of the land, participating in cattle mustering and sleeping under the star-studded Outback sky, gaining a profound appreciation for the vastness and untamed spirit of the Australian wilderness.

From the untamed Outback, James headed towards the pristine Whitsunday Islands. Sailing through the turquoise waters, he discovered secluded beaches and secret coves that took his breath away. Walking on the pure white sands of Whitehaven Beach, he felt the softness beneath his feet, a sensation he would forever associate with paradise.

As his Queensland adventure neared its end, James reflected on the diversity of experiences he had encountered. From the vibrant city life to the awe-inspiring wonders of the reef, rainforest, and outback, he had witnessed the true essence of Queensland. With memories etched in his heart, James bid farewell to this extraordinary land, grateful for the personal growth and unforgettable moments that had shaped his fictional exploration of Queensland in 2023.

INTRODUCTION TO QUEENSLAND

WELCOME TO QUEENSLAND

Queensland is a state in northeastern Australia, known as the "Sunshine State" due to its abundant sunshine and warm climate. It is the second-largest state in Australia and offers a diverse range of attractions for visitors.

The capital city of Queensland is Brisbane, a vibrant and cosmopolitan city situated on the banks of the Brisbane River. Brisbane is known for its modern skyline, cultural events, and a thriving dining and nightlife scene.

One of the highlights of Queensland is the Great Barrier Reef, the largest coral reef system in the world. This UNESCO World Heritage site stretches along the state's coastline and offers incredible opportunities for snorkelling, scuba diving, and marine exploration.

The state is also famous for its beautiful beaches, including Surfers Paradise on the Gold Coast and the Sunshine Coast. These coastal regions are perfect for swimming, surfing, and sunbathing.

For nature lovers, Queensland offers stunning national parks and natural wonders. The Daintree Rainforest, the oldest tropical rainforest in the world, is a haven for biodiversity, with unique flora and fauna. The Whitsunday Islands, with their pristine beaches and clear waters, are a paradise for sailing, snorkelling, and relaxation.

Inland Queensland showcases the Australian outback, with vast plains, rugged mountains, and iconic landmarks like Uluru (Ayers Rock). Exploring the outback provides an opportunity to experience the unique landscapes and learn about Aboriginal culture.

Queensland hosts a range of events and festivals throughout the year, including the Brisbane Festival and the Woodford Folk Festival. These celebrations showcase the state's rich arts, culture, and culinary offerings.

Adventure enthusiasts can indulge in activities like skydiving, bungee jumping, and white-water rafting. Queensland also boasts world-class theme parks, such as Dreamworld and SeaWorld, providing thrills and entertainment for all ages.

With its diverse landscapes, natural wonders, cultural experiences, and vibrant cities, Queensland offers something for everyone. Whether you seek relaxation on stunning beaches, outdoor adventures in the wilderness, or cultural immersion in vibrant cities, Queensland welcomes you with its warmth, beauty, and unique charm.

GEOGRAPHY AND CLIMATE

Geography:

Queensland is located in northeastern Australia and covers a vast area of approximately 1.85 million square kilometres. It is the second-largest state in Australia, surpassed only by Western Australia. The state is bordered by the Coral Sea and the Pacific Ocean to the east, and it shares borders with the Northern Territory, South Australia, and New South Wales.

The geography of Queensland is incredibly diverse. It features stunning coastal regions, including the iconic Great Barrier Reef, which stretches over

2,300 kilometres along the northeastern coastline. The coastline is dotted with beautiful beaches, vibrant seaside towns, and popular tourist destinations like the Gold Coast and the Sunshine Coast.

Moving inland, Queensland encompasses vast expanses of the Australian outback. This includes arid plains, rugged mountain ranges, and expansive deserts. The state is also home to lush tropical rainforests, such as the Daintree Rainforest, which is considered the oldest rainforest on Earth.

Several major river systems flow through Queensland, including the Fitzroy, the Burnett, and the mighty Queensland's longest river, the 1,413-kilometre-long Flinders River.

Climate:

Queensland's climate varies significantly across its vast expanse. In the coastal regions, including Brisbane and the Gold Coast, the climate is generally subtropical, with hot and humid summers and mild, dry winters. Average summer temperatures range from 25 to 30 degrees Celsius (77 to 86 degrees Fahrenheit), while winter temperatures hover around 15 to 25 degrees Celsius (59 to 77 degrees Fahrenheit).

As you move further inland, the climate becomes more arid and experiences a semi-arid or desert climate in some areas. Summers can be scorching hot, with temperatures exceeding 40 degrees Celsius (104 degrees Fahrenheit), while winters are colder but still warm during the day.

In the far north of Queensland, the region known as the Tropical North experiences a tropical climate with high humidity and distinct wet and dry seasons. The wet season, usually occurring from November to April, brings heavy rainfall and occasional tropical cyclones. The dry season, from May to October, offers milder temperatures and lower humidity.

It's important to note that due to its vast size, Queensland's climate can vary greatly depending on the specific location within the state. It's always advisable to check the weather and climate patterns of the specific region you plan to visit.

Overall, Queensland's diverse geography and climate make it a unique destination, offering a wide range of landscapes and outdoor experiences for visitors to enjoy.

QUEENSLAND CULTURE AND HISTORY

Culture:

Queensland is a state in Australia with a vibrant and diverse culture that celebrates its rich history, indigenous heritage, arts, sports, and culinary traditions.

Indigenous Culture: Queensland is home to various indigenous communities, including Aboriginal and Torres Strait Islander peoples. Their cultural heritage is deeply rooted in the land, and visitors can learn about their ancient traditions, Dreamtime stories, art, music, and dance.

Arts and Festivals: Queensland has a thriving arts scene, with numerous galleries, theatres, and festivals. The state hosts events like the Brisbane Festival, showcasing music, dance, theatre, and visual arts. The Woodford Folk Festival is a renowned celebration of music, culture, and ideas.

Sports Culture: Queenslanders are passionate about sports, particularly rugby league. The state supports teams like the Brisbane Broncos and the North Queensland Cowboys. The State of Origin, a rugby league series between Queensland and New South Wales, is a highly anticipated sporting event.

Culinary Delights: Queensland offers a diverse culinary experience influenced by its multicultural population. Visitors can savour fresh seafood, tropical fruits, and farm-fresh produce. The state is known for its seafood, barbecues, and international cuisine.

History:

Queensland has a rich history shaped by its indigenous heritage and European settlement.

Indigenous Heritage: Aboriginal and Torres Strait Islander peoples have a deep connection to the land, with a cultural history dating back thousands of years. Visitors can explore rock art sites, learn about indigenous traditions, and appreciate their spiritual connection to the natural environment.

European Settlement: Queensland was explored by Dutch and British navigators. The Moreton Bay Penal Settlement, established in 1824, evolved into Brisbane. In 1859, Queensland separated from New South Wales and became a self-governing colony.

Gold Rush and Development: The late 19th century brought a gold rush, leading to rapid growth. Gold discoveries in places like Gympie and Mount Morgan attracted prospectors, contributing to the state's economic development.

World War II: During World War II, Queensland played a crucial role in defending Australia. The state served as a base for Allied forces, and cities like Townsville and Cairns were significant military outposts in the Pacific.

Queensland's culture and history are showcased through heritage sites, museums, and landmarks, offering insights into its past. Exploring these places provides a deeper understanding of the state's development and the contributions of its diverse communities.

Queensland's culture is a tapestry of indigenous traditions, artistic expression, sporting enthusiasm, and culinary delights. Its history is a fascinating journey of indigenous heritage, European settlement, gold rushes, and wartime contributions.

TRAVEL ESSENTIALS

Travel Essentials for Queensland:

1. Visa Requirements: Check the visa requirements for entering Australia and ensure you have the appropriate visa before your trip.

2. Passport: Make sure your passport is valid for at least six months beyond your intended stay in Queensland.

3. Travel Insurance: It is highly recommended to have travel insurance that covers medical emergencies, trip cancellations, and lost or stolen belongings.

4. Health and Vaccinations: Check with your doctor or a travel health clinic for any recommended vaccinations or health precautions for visiting Queensland.

5. Weather and Clothing: Queensland has a varied climate, so pack clothing suitable for the weather conditions during your visit. Include swimwear, light clothing for warm weather, and a light jacket or sweater for cooler evenings.

6. Sun Protection: Queensland is known for its sunshine, so pack sunscreen, a hat, sunglasses, and protective clothing to shield yourself from the sun's rays.

7. Insect Repellent: Insect repellent is advisable, especially in tropical regions, to protect against mosquitoes and other insects.

8. Currency: The currency in Australia is the Australian Dollar (AUD). Ensure you have adequate cash or a credit/debit card widely accepted in the country.

9. Power Adapters: The electrical voltage in Australia is 230V, and the plug type is Type I. Bring a universal power adapter if your devices use different plug types.

10. Transportation: Research transportation options within Queensland, including flights, trains, buses, and car rentals, depending on your travel plans.

11. Safety and Security: Queensland is generally safe, but it's always wise to take precautions. Be aware of your surroundings, secure your belongings, and follow local safety guidelines.

12. Communication: Check with your mobile service provider about international roaming or consider purchasing a local SIM card for data and calling purposes during your stay.

13. Itinerary and Reservations: Plan your itinerary and make necessary reservations for accommodation, tours, and attractions in advance, particularly during peak travel seasons.

14. Local Customs: Familiarise yourself with local customs and etiquette to respect the local culture and traditions.

15. COVID-19 Considerations: Stay informed about travel restrictions, health protocols, and any specific requirements related to COVID-19 for entering and travelling within Queensland. Follow the guidelines provided by health authorities.

Always check the latest travel advisories and guidelines from your home country and the Australian government to ensure a smooth and enjoyable visit to Queensland.

PLANNING YOUR TRIP TO QUEENSLAND

BEST TIME TO VISIT QUEENSLAND

Queensland, located in northeastern Australia, offers a diverse range of attractions, including stunning beaches, tropical rainforests, vibrant cities, and the iconic Great Barrier Reef. To make the most of your trip to Queensland, it's important to consider the best time to visit. Here's a detailed and short information guide to help you plan your trip:

1. Seasons in Queensland:
   - Summer (December to February): Hot and humid with occasional tropical storms.
   - Autumn (March to May): Warm temperatures with reduced rainfall.
   - Winter (June to August): Mild and dry weather, particularly in the southern regions.

- Spring (September to November): Increasing temperatures and humidity, occasional showers.

2. Best Time to Visit Queensland:
The best time to visit Queensland is during the autumn (March to May) and spring (September to November) seasons. These months offer pleasant temperatures, lower humidity, and less rainfall, making it ideal for outdoor activities and sightseeing.

3. Great Barrier Reef:
For visiting the Great Barrier Reef, the best time is between May and November. During this period, water visibility is excellent, and you can witness the annual coral spawning between October and November.

4. Queensland's Tropical North:
If you plan to explore the tropical regions of Queensland, such as Cairns and the Daintree Rainforest, the dry season (June to October) is preferred. This period offers comfortable temperatures, minimal rainfall, and excellent conditions for outdoor activities.

5. Whale Watching:

From June to November, Queensland's coast offers fantastic whale watching opportunities, as humpback whales migrate along the coastline. Locations like Hervey Bay, Gold Coast, and Whitsundays provide excellent viewing opportunities.

6. School Holidays and Peak Seasons:

Consider school holidays and major events when planning your trip, as they can affect crowds and prices. Queensland's school holidays generally occur in late March, June-July, September, and December-January. Major events like the Brisbane Festival (September) and the Gold Coast 600 V8 Supercars race (October) attract many visitors.

Remember to check specific weather forecasts and regional considerations for the destinations you plan to visit in Queensland. This information will help you make the most informed decision based on your preferences and desired activities.

VISA AND ENTRY REQUIREMENTS

If you're planning a trip to Queensland, Australia, it's important to understand the visa and entry requirements. Here's a detailed and concise overview to help you plan your visit:

1. Visa Requirements:
   Most visitors to Australia require a visa. The type of visa you need depends on your nationality and the purpose and duration of your visit. Common visa types for tourists include the Electronic Travel Authority (ETA) Subclass 601, eVisitor Subclass 651, and Visitor Visa Subclass 600.

2. Passport Validity:
   Ensure your passport is valid for at least six months beyond your intended departure date from Australia.

3. Online Application:

Apply for an ETA or eVisitor visa online through the Australian Department of Home Affairs website or authorised agents.

4. Medical Requirements:
Some visitors may need a medical examination or vaccinations based on travel history and circumstances.

5. Customs and Quarantine:
Declare restricted items like food, animal products, and plant material on arrival to comply with Australia's strict regulations.

6. COVID-19 Travel Restrictions:
Check the latest travel advisories, entry requirements, and quarantine regulations related to COVID-19 before planning your trip.

7. Other Considerations:
Obtain travel insurance, show proof of sufficient funds, and have a return or onward ticket.

Remember to check official government websites or consult with the nearest Australian embassy or consulate for the most up-to-date and accurate information regarding visa and entry requirements for Queensland.

TRAVEL INSURANCE

When planning a trip to Queensland, Australia, it's crucial to consider travel insurance to protect yourself and your belongings. Here's a detailed and concise overview of travel insurance for your Queensland trip:

1. Importance of Travel Insurance:
   Travel insurance provides financial protection against unforeseen events and emergencies that can occur during your trip. It covers medical expenses, trip cancellations, lost belongings, and other travel-related risks.

2. Coverage Options:
   Travel insurance policies typically offer various coverage options, including:

- Medical expenses: Covers healthcare costs, hospitalisation, and emergency medical evacuation.
- Trip cancellation or interruption: Reimburses non-refundable expenses if your trip is cancelled or cut short due to covered reasons.
- Baggage and personal belongings: Provides compensation for lost, stolen, or damaged luggage and personal items.
- Travel delays: Offers compensation for additional expenses incurred due to travel delays or missed connections.
- Personal liability: Covers legal expenses if you cause injury or damage to others during your trip.
- Emergency assistance: Provides access to 24/7 assistance services for emergencies and travel-related information.

3. Choosing a Policy:
   When selecting travel insurance:
- Assess your needs: Consider the activities you'll be doing and the level of coverage required.
- Read policy details: Understand coverage limits, exclusions, and any pre-existing condition clauses.

- Compare quotes and coverage: Obtain quotes from different providers and compare coverage and premiums.

- Check exclusions: Be aware of activities, destinations, or circumstances not covered by the policy.

4. Pre-Existing Medical Conditions:

Declare any pre-existing medical conditions when purchasing travel insurance. Some policies may cover these conditions, while others may require additional premiums or exclusions.

5. Emergency Contact Information:

Keep a copy of your travel insurance policy and emergency contact details with you during your trip.

6. Additional Considerations:

- Check existing coverage: Review if your credit card or health insurance provides travel insurance benefits.

- Adventure activities: Ensure your insurance covers any adventure sports or activities you plan to participate in.

- Read reviews and research: Look for reputable insurance providers and read customer reviews for reliability and customer service.

Remember to review policy terms, ask questions for clarification, and choose travel insurance that suits your needs and provides adequate coverage for your Queensland trip.

BUDGETING AND MONEY MATTERS

When planning a trip to Queensland, Australia, it's crucial to consider budgeting and money matters to ensure a smooth and enjoyable experience. Here's a detailed and concise overview to help you plan your finances for your Queensland trip:

1. Currency:
   The official currency in Australia is the Australian Dollar (AUD). Exchange your currency to AUD before your trip or use ATMs or currency exchange services in Queensland.

2. Cost of Living:

Queensland's cost of living can vary depending on the region and type of accommodation. Major cities like Brisbane generally have higher prices compared to smaller towns or rural areas.

3. Accommodation:

Accommodation costs vary based on the type and location. Options include hotels, motels, hostels, serviced apartments, and camping grounds. Research and compare prices to find the best deals.

4. Dining:

Dining costs can vary depending on the type of restaurant or eatery. Queensland offers a range of dining options, from budget-friendly cafes to upscale restaurants. Consider trying local markets and street food to save money.

5. Transportation:

Allocate a budget for transportation, including flights, airport transfers, and local transportation within Queensland. Public transportation such as buses, trains, or trams is often more affordable than taxis or rental cars.

6. Activities and Attractions:

Research the costs of activities and attractions you plan to visit in Queensland. Some attractions may have entrance fees or require advanced bookings. Look for any available discounts or combo packages.

7. Travel Insurance:

Include travel insurance in your budget to protect yourself against unforeseen events and emergencies. Compare different policies to find the one that suits your needs.

8. Tipping:

Tipping is not as common in Australia as it is in some other countries. While not mandatory, you can leave a small tip for exceptional service if you wish to do so.

9. Taxes:

Goods and Services Tax (GST) of 10% applies to most goods and services in Australia. Account for this when budgeting for purchases.

10. Payment Options:

Credit cards are widely accepted in Queensland, but it's advisable to carry some cash for smaller establishments and markets. Notify your bank of your travel plans to avoid any issues with your cards.

11. Emergency Funds:

Set aside some emergency funds for unexpected expenses or situations that may arise during your trip.

Remember to plan and monitor your expenses, prioritise your spending based on your preferences, and allocate your budget wisely to make the most of your trip to Queensland.

TRANSPORTATION IN QUEENSLAND

When planning a trip to Queensland, Australia, it's important to consider transportation options to navigate the state. Here's a detailed and concise overview of transportation in Queensland:

1. Air Travel:
   Queensland has several airports, with Brisbane Airport being the busiest. It offers domestic and international flights. Regional airports serve popular destinations like Cairns, Gold Coast, and Townsville.

2. Public Transportation:
   - Buses: Queensland has an extensive bus network, especially in urban areas like Brisbane, Gold Coast, and Cairns. TransLink operates buses in South East Queensland, while regional towns have their own services.
   - Trains: Queensland Rail operates train services connecting major cities and regional areas.

Long-distance options include the Tilt Train and Spirit of Queensland.

3. Ferries:
Coastal regions and islands, such as the Great Barrier Reef and Moreton Bay, provide ferry services for transportation and scenic experiences.

4. Rental Cars:
Renting a car offers flexibility for exploring Queensland. Rental car companies are available at airports, cities, and tourist destinations. Check driving permit requirements and local traffic rules.

5. Taxis and Ride-Sharing:
Taxis are available in cities and larger towns, and ride-sharing services like Uber operate in major urban areas.

6. Regional and Outback Travel:
For remote areas or the Queensland outback, consider 4WD tours, guided trips, or hiring suitable vehicles. Ensure you're well-prepared and informed about road conditions and safety requirements.

7. Cycling and Walking:

Queensland provides cycling paths and walking trails in many areas, offering an eco-friendly and scenic way to explore cities, coastal regions, and national parks.

8. Tourist Shuttles and Transfers:

Many tourist destinations in Queensland offer shuttle services or transfers between popular attractions, airports, and accommodation, providing convenience for tourists.

9. Accessibility:

Major transportation services, airports, and public transport systems in Queensland aim to provide accessibility for individuals with disabilities. Wheelchair-accessible facilities are available on many buses and trains.

10. Traffic and Peak Times:

Major cities like Brisbane can experience heavy traffic during peak hours, so plan your travel accordingly and allow extra time during rush hours.

Remember to plan your transportation in advance, consider the distance between destinations, and use travel apps, official websites, and visitor information centres for up-to-date schedules and information. This will help you make the most of your trip to Queensland.

ACCOMMODATION OPTIONS

When planning a trip to Queensland, Australia, it's important to consider accommodation options that suit your needs and preferences. Here's a detailed and concise overview of accommodation options in Queensland:

1. Hotels and Resorts:
   Queensland offers a wide range of hotels and resorts catering to different budgets and preferences. From luxury five-star resorts to budget-friendly accommodations, you'll find options in major cities, coastal areas, and tourist destinations.

2. Motels:

Motels are a popular choice for budget-conscious travellers. They provide basic amenities and are often located along highways or in smaller towns.

3. Serviced Apartments:

Serviced apartments offer the comforts of home with the convenience of hotel services. They typically include a kitchenette or full kitchen, living area, and separate bedrooms.

4. Holiday Homes and Vacation Rentals:

Queensland has many holiday homes and vacation rentals available for short-term stays. These options are ideal for families or larger groups, offering more space and privacy.

5. Hostels:

Hostels provide affordable accommodation, especially for solo travellers or backpackers. They offer shared dormitory rooms or private rooms, along with common areas and facilities for socialising.

6. Caravan Parks and Camping Grounds:

If you're travelling with a caravan or enjoy camping, Queensland has numerous caravan parks and camping grounds. These are often located near beaches, national parks, and scenic areas.

7. Bed and Breakfasts (B&Bs):
B&Bs are a charming accommodation option, particularly in smaller towns and rural areas. They offer comfortable rooms and a homemade breakfast.

8. Eco-Resorts and Eco-Lodges:
For those seeking sustainable and eco-friendly accommodation, Queensland has eco-resorts and eco-lodges nestled in natural surroundings. These properties prioritise environmental conservation and offer unique experiences.

9. Farm Stays:
Experience rural life in Queensland by opting for a farm stay. You can stay on working farms and participate in activities like animal feeding or horse riding.

10. Indigenous Cultural Experiences:

Queensland provides opportunities for immersive Indigenous cultural experiences, including accommodations in Indigenous-owned and operated lodges or campsites.

11. Online Booking Platforms:

Utilise online platforms such as hotel booking websites, vacation rental websites, or tourism websites to search and book accommodations in Queensland.

Remember to consider factors such as location, amenities, proximity to attractions, and your budget when choosing accommodation in Queensland. Booking in advance is recommended, especially during peak travel seasons or for popular destinations.

BRISBANE AND SURROUNDING REGIONS

EXPLORING BRISBANE CITY

Brisbane, the capital city of Queensland, offers a dynamic urban experience with a blend of cultural, natural, and culinary attractions. Here's a detailed and concise overview of exploring Brisbane city and its surrounding regions:

1. South Bank Parklands:
   South Bank Parklands is a riverside oasis featuring lush gardens, picnic areas, and the man-made Streets Beach. Enjoy swimming, strolling along the promenade, visiting art galleries, or dining at the diverse range of restaurants and cafes.

2. Brisbane City Botanic Gardens:
   Located near the CBD, the City Botanic Gardens is a serene haven for nature lovers. Take a leisurely walk amidst beautifully landscaped gardens, enjoy

the river views, or have a picnic under the shade of tall trees.

3. Cultural Precinct:

The South Bank Cultural Precinct is home to world-class institutions like the Queensland Museum, Queensland Art Gallery, Gallery of Modern Art, and State Library of Queensland. Explore art, history, science, and literature through their engaging exhibitions and events.

4. Queen Street Mall:

Queen Street Mall is a vibrant shopping hub in the heart of the city. Discover a wide range of retail stores, department stores, and boutiques. Enjoy street performances, dine at cafes and restaurants, or catch a movie at the nearby cinema.

5. Kangaroo Point Cliffs:

Kangaroo Point Cliffs offer panoramic views of the city skyline and Brisbane River. Take a scenic walk, try rock climbing, or have a riverside picnic while enjoying the breathtaking scenery.

6. Lone Pine Koala Sanctuary:

Lone Pine Koala Sanctuary is a must-visit for wildlife enthusiasts. Get up close with koalas, hand-feed kangaroos, and encounter various Australian animals. Watch animal shows and learn about conservation efforts.

7. Moreton Island:

Embark on a day trip or overnight adventure to Moreton Island, located off the coast of Brisbane. Enjoy snorkelling, swimming, and sandboarding on the island's pristine beaches. Don't miss the chance to spot dolphins and explore the Tangalooma Wrecks.

8. Mount Coot-tha:

Mount Coot-tha offers panoramic views of Brisbane from its lookout point. Visit the Brisbane Botanic Gardens at the base, have a meal at the Summit Restaurant, or go for bushwalks in the surrounding area.

9. Brisbane River Cruise:

Experience Brisbane from the water by taking a scenic river cruise. Cruise along the river, passing iconic landmarks like the Story Bridge and the City

Botanic Gardens. Enjoy informative commentary and soak in the city's beauty.

10. Eat Street Northshore:

Indulge in a unique dining experience at Eat Street Northshore, a vibrant night market featuring an array of food stalls, live music, and a lively atmosphere. Sample a variety of cuisines and enjoy the vibrant ambiance.

Explore Brisbane's diverse neighbourhoods, immerse yourself in its cultural scene, and savour the city's culinary delights to make the most of your visit to this dynamic Australian city.

SOUTH BANK PARKLANDS

South Bank Parklands is a vibrant and popular destination located on the southern bank of the Brisbane River. Here's a detailed and concise overview of exploring South Bank Parklands:

1. Streets Beach:

Enjoy a unique beach experience in the heart of the city at Streets Beach. This man-made beach features white sand, palm trees, and a sparkling lagoon. Swim, sunbathe, or relax under the shade of the pandanus trees.

2. Parklands and Gardens:

South Bank Parklands offers spacious parklands and beautifully landscaped gardens. Take a leisurely walk along the riverfront promenade, have a picnic on the grassy lawns, or simply unwind amidst the peaceful surroundings.

3. Cultural Institutions:

South Bank is home to several cultural institutions, including the Queensland Museum, Queensland Art Gallery, and Gallery of Modern Art (QAGOMA). Explore art, history, and exhibitions that showcase local and international works.

4. Wheel of Brisbane:

Take a ride on the iconic Wheel of Brisbane for stunning panoramic views of the city skyline. Step into the air-conditioned gondolas and enjoy a 360-degree view from the top.

5. Dining and Shopping:

South Bank offers a diverse range of dining options, from casual eateries to fine dining restaurants. Sample cuisine from around the world and enjoy alfresco dining along the riverfront. Explore the nearby markets and boutique shops for unique finds.

6. Aquativity:

Aquativity is a water playground that provides interactive water play for kids of all ages. Let the little ones splash around in the fountains, water jets, and shallow pools.

7. Riverside Walk and Cycling Tracks:

Take a leisurely stroll or bike ride along the riverside paths that wind through the South Bank. Enjoy the scenic views, spot public artworks, and soak in the lively atmosphere.

8. Events and Festivals:

South Bank hosts various events and festivals throughout the year, including cultural celebrations, live music performances, and food markets. Check the calendar to see what's happening during your visit.

South Bank Parklands is a bustling and lively precinct that offers a mix of natural beauty, cultural experiences, and recreational activities. Whether you want to relax on the beach, explore art galleries, or indulge in delicious food, South Bank has something for everyone to enjoy.

QUEENSLAND MUSEUM AND GALLERY OF MODERN ART

The Queensland Museum and the Gallery of Modern Art (QAGOMA) are two prominent cultural institutions in Brisbane. Here's a detailed and concise overview of these attractions:

1. Queensland Museum:
   The Queensland Museum is a fascinating destination that showcases the natural and cultural history of Queensland. Explore exhibits on dinosaurs, ancient civilizations, indigenous

cultures, and the biodiversity of the region. Learn about the Great Barrier Reef, Queensland's unique wildlife, and the impact of environmental changes.

2. Gallery of Modern Art (QAGOMA):
The Gallery of Modern Art is a premier art museum that houses an impressive collection of contemporary artworks. Discover thought-provoking exhibitions featuring paintings, sculptures, installations, photography, and multimedia pieces. QAGOMA also hosts travelling exhibitions from around the world, showcasing diverse artistic perspectives.

3. Exhibitions and Collections:
Both the Queensland Museum and QAGOMA offer a rotating schedule of exhibitions that cater to various interests. The Queensland Museum's collections range from fossils and natural history specimens to cultural artefacts. QAGOMA's collections span modern and contemporary art, with a focus on Australian and Indigenous works.

4. Children's Activities:

The Queensland Museum and QAGOMA provide engaging activities and exhibitions for children. From interactive displays and hands-on experiments to dedicated kids' areas, young visitors can learn while having fun. Check their websites for specific programs and events designed for children.

5. Special Events and Programs:

Both institutions host a range of special events, including artist talks, workshops, film screenings, and performances. These events offer unique opportunities to engage with artists, experts, and cultural practitioners. Stay updated on their event calendars for upcoming programs.

6. Dining and Facilities:

The Queensland Museum and QAGOMA feature on-site cafes and restaurants where visitors can enjoy refreshments and meals. Additionally, gift shops and bookstores offer a selection of art-related merchandise, books, and souvenirs. The facilities include amenities for a comfortable and enjoyable visit.

7. Location and Access:

The Queensland Museum is located in South Bank, near the Brisbane CBD. QAGOMA is situated adjacent to the Queensland Museum, making it convenient to visit both attractions in one trip. Public transportation options, including buses, trains, and ferries, provide easy access to the area.

Visiting the Queensland Museum and QAGOMA allows you to immerse yourself in the rich cultural and artistic offerings of Brisbane. Whether you're interested in natural history, contemporary art, or Indigenous culture, these institutions provide engaging and enlightening experiences for visitors of all ages.

LONE PINE KOALA SANCTUARY

Lone Pine Koala Sanctuary is a popular attraction located in the outskirts of Brisbane, Queensland. Here's a detailed and concise overview of Lone Pine Koala Sanctuary:

1. Koala Encounters:

Lone Pine offers the opportunity to meet and interact with koalas. You can hold a koala, have your photo taken, and learn about these iconic Australian animals.

2. Australian Wildlife:

Explore the sanctuary to encounter a wide variety of native Australian wildlife. From kangaroos and wallabies to wombats and dingoes, you can observe and learn about the diverse species that call Australia home.

3. Wildlife Shows and Presentations:

Enjoy entertaining and educational wildlife shows and presentations. Watch sheepdog shows, raptor displays, and snake handling demonstrations by experienced handlers.

4. Platypus House:

Visit the Platypus House to see the elusive and unique platypus. Learn about their habits and behaviours while observing them in specially designed enclosures.

5. Free-Flight Bird Show:

Witness the beauty and intelligence of native Australian birds in the Free-Flight Bird Show. Colourful parrots and cockatoos showcase their skills and perform in a free-flight demonstration.

6. Kangaroo Feeding:
Participate in kangaroo feeding sessions and hand-feed these gentle creatures. Learn about their biology and behaviour while interacting with them up close.

7. Eucalyptus Forest and Picnic Areas:
Lone Pine is nestled in a serene eucalyptus forest, providing a peaceful setting. Take a stroll through the forest, relax in the picnic areas, and enjoy the natural beauty of the surroundings.

8. Facilities:
Lone Pine Koala Sanctuary offers various amenities, including a café where you can grab a bite to eat, as well as a souvenir shop where you can find Australian-themed gifts and koala souvenirs.

Lone Pine Koala Sanctuary is a fantastic place to get acquainted with Australia's unique wildlife. Whether you're cuddling a koala, hand-feeding kangaroos, or watching captivating wildlife shows, the sanctuary offers an enjoyable and educational experience for visitors of all ages.

MORETON BAY ISLANDS

The Moreton Bay Islands are a group of beautiful islands located near Brisbane, offering a range of natural attractions and recreational activities. Here's a detailed and concise overview of the Moreton Bay Islands:

1. North Stradbroke Island:
   North Stradbroke Island, or "Straddie," is the largest of the Moreton Bay Islands. It features stunning beaches, freshwater lakes, and scenic walks. Enjoy swimming, surfing, fishing, and wildlife spotting. The island is also known for its annual whale migration, offering excellent opportunities for whale watching.

2. Moreton Island:

Moreton Island is a popular destination for day trips and camping adventures. It boasts picturesque sand dunes, clear waters, and an abundance of marine life. Engage in activities like sandboarding, snorkelling around the Tangalooma Wrecks, and swimming in the Champagne Pools.

3. Bribie Island:

Bribie Island is the closest Moreton Bay Island to Brisbane and offers a relaxed coastal getaway. Enjoy sandy beaches, explore the Pumicestone Passage by kayak or boat, and discover the diverse wildlife in the Bribie Island National Park. The island also features a golf course, fishing spots, and charming seaside villages.

4. Coochiemudlo Island:

Coochiemudlo Island is a small and peaceful island known for its laid-back atmosphere. Relax on the sandy shores, go for a swim, or take a leisurely stroll around the island. Enjoy picnics in the parklands and soak in the tranquillity of this hidden gem.

5. Outdoor Activities:

The Moreton Bay Islands offer a range of outdoor activities. From swimming and beachcombing to kayaking and snorkelling, there's something for everyone. Explore nature trails, go birdwatching, or try your hand at fishing in the surrounding waters.

6. Camping and Accommodation:

Camping facilities are available on North Stradbroke Island and Moreton Island, providing an opportunity to immerse yourself in nature. Additionally, there are holiday houses, resorts, and camping grounds available for those seeking a comfortable stay.

7. Tours and Excursions:

Various tour operators offer guided tours and excursions to the Moreton Bay Islands. Join a guided eco-tour, dolphin-watching cruise, or cultural experience to enhance your island adventure.

The Moreton Bay Islands offer a diverse range of natural beauty, outdoor activities, and opportunities for relaxation. Whether you're seeking adventure, wildlife encounters, or a peaceful retreat, these islands provide a scenic and accessible escape from the city of Brisbane.

GOLD COAST

SURFERS PARADISE

Gold Coast: Surfers Paradise is a vibrant coastal suburb in Queensland, Australia, known for its stunning beaches, lively atmosphere, and iconic skyline. Situated on the east coast, Surfers Paradise is part of the larger Gold Coast region, which is a popular tourist destination.

The suburb's main attraction is its beautiful beach, with golden sands and rolling waves that attract surfers, swimmers, and sun-seekers. The beach is patrolled by lifeguards, ensuring a safe environment for visitors.

Surfers Paradise is famous for its high-rise buildings that line the beachfront, offering stunning views of the Pacific Ocean. The area is known for its modern architecture and skyline, which is particularly impressive when viewed from the water or the SkyPoint Observation Deck.

Cavill Avenue is the main street of Surfers Paradise, bustling with activity. It is a pedestrian mall filled with an array of shops, boutiques, restaurants, cafes, and bars. Visitors can enjoy shopping for fashion, souvenirs, and local crafts, or indulge in a wide variety of dining options.

At night, Surfers Paradise comes alive with its vibrant nightlife. The suburb boasts numerous nightclubs, bars, and entertainment venues that cater to a diverse range of tastes. Visitors can dance the night away, enjoy live music performances, or simply relax with a cocktail while taking in the energetic atmosphere.

Surfers Paradise is also home to several popular attractions. The SkyPoint Observation Deck, located in the Q1 Building, provides panoramic views of the Gold Coast skyline and the surrounding area. The beach itself offers opportunities for water sports, such as surfing, jet-skiing, and parasailing.

For families, the suburb offers a variety of theme parks nearby, including Dreamworld, Sea World,

Warner Bros. Movie World, and Wet'n'Wild. These parks feature thrilling rides, entertaining shows, and interactive experiences suitable for all ages.

Throughout the year, Surfers Paradise hosts various events and festivals, ranging from sporting events to music festivals and cultural celebrations. These events add to the vibrant atmosphere of the suburb and provide additional entertainment options for visitors.

In summary, Surfers Paradise is a bustling and exciting coastal suburb in the Gold Coast, offering stunning beaches, a lively nightlife, diverse shopping and dining experiences, and a range of attractions and events. It is a destination that caters to all types of travellers, from beach lovers to adventure seekers, making it a popular choice for visitors from around the world.

THEME PARKS (DREAMWORLD, WARNER BROS. MOVIE WORLD, SEA WORLD)

Gold Coast is renowned for its thrilling theme parks, offering a variety of exciting experiences for visitors of all ages. Three popular theme parks in the area are Dreamworld, Warner Bros. Movie World, and SeaWorld.

Dreamworld is the largest theme park in Australia and offers a diverse range of attractions. It features adrenaline-pumping rides, such as the Tower of Terror II and the BuzzSaw roller coaster, as well as family-friendly rides like the Pandemonium and The Wiggles World. Dreamworld is also home to Tiger Island, where visitors can see tigers and experience thrilling wildlife presentations. Additionally, the park has interactive animal encounters, live shows, and a water park called WhiteWater World.

Warner Bros. Movie World combines the excitement of a theme park with the magic of movies. Visitors can enjoy thrilling rides inspired by famous movies, such as the DC Rivals HyperCoaster and the Justice League 3D dark ride. Movie World also offers entertaining shows, including the Hollywood Stunt Driver 2 show and the Star Parade. Guests can meet their favourite Warner Bros. characters, including Batman, Superman, and Wonder Woman. The park provides an immersive cinematic experience, making visitors feel like they are part of the action.

Sea World is a marine-themed park that combines entertainment with education. It offers a variety of marine animal encounters, including the opportunity to see dolphins, seals, and penguins up close. The park features shows and presentations, such as the Dolphin Presentation and the Jet Stunt Extreme show. Sea World also offers exciting rides, including the Storm Coaster and the Jet Rescue roller coaster. In addition to the animal experiences and rides, Sea World has an interactive water play area called Castaway Bay.

These theme parks provide a wide range of attractions, rides, shows, and interactive experiences, ensuring there is something for everyone. Each park has its unique theme and focus, offering visitors a chance to immerse themselves in thrilling adventures, movie magic, or marine life exploration. Whether you are seeking adrenaline-pumping rides, live shows, animal encounters, or a mix of everything, the Gold Coast theme parks are sure to provide a memorable and fun-filled experience for all visitors.

BURLEIGH HEADS AND GOLD COAST HINTERLAND

Gold Coast: Burleigh Heads is a picturesque coastal suburb located in the southern part of the Gold Coast in Queensland, Australia. Known for its natural beauty, Burleigh Heads offers a combination of stunning beaches, lush parklands, and a laid-back atmosphere.

The suburb's main attraction is Burleigh Beach, a pristine stretch of sand that is popular for swimming, surfing, and beachside picnics. The beach is surrounded by Burleigh Headland, a national park that offers walking trails with panoramic views of the coastline and the opportunity to spot wildlife, including native birds and sometimes even dolphins and whales.

Burleigh Heads is also home to the Burleigh Heads National Park, which features rainforest walks, scenic lookouts, and a renowned surfing point break known as "The Point." Visitors can explore the park's walking trails, admire the coastal views, and enjoy a picnic amidst the natural surroundings.

The suburb itself has a vibrant and relaxed atmosphere, with a thriving café and dining scene. James Street is a popular destination for food lovers, offering a range of trendy cafes, restaurants, and boutique shops. Visitors can indulge in delicious meals, sip on artisan coffee, and browse unique stores for local fashion and crafts.

In addition to the coastal attractions, the Gold Coast Hinterland is a scenic and verdant region located just a short drive inland from the coast. It is characterised by lush rainforests, waterfalls, and charming mountain villages. Some notable destinations in the Gold Coast Hinterland include Springbrook National Park, Lamington National Park, and Mount Tamborine.

Springbrook National Park is known for its cascading waterfalls, ancient forests, and breathtaking lookouts. Visitors can explore the park's walking trails, swim in natural rock pools, and witness the mesmerising glow worms at night.

Lamington National Park is part of the Gondwana Rainforests of Australia World Heritage Area and offers a diverse range of flora and fauna. It is renowned for its hiking trails, including the popular Border Track, and for its birdwatching opportunities.

Mount Tamborine is a charming mountain village that is famous for its boutique wineries, art galleries, and breathtaking views of the surrounding hinterland. Visitors can indulge in wine tasting, explore the village's quaint shops, and enjoy nature walks through the rainforest.

The Gold Coast Hinterland provides a serene and natural escape from the coastal hustle and bustle, offering visitors a chance to immerse themselves in the region's stunning landscapes and relax in a tranquil setting.

Overall, Burleigh Heads and the Gold Coast Hinterland offer a diverse range of attractions, from pristine beaches and coastal walks to lush rainforests and charming mountain villages. Whether you seek sun and surf or a peaceful retreat in nature, this region of the Gold Coast has something to offer every visitor.

LAMINGTON NATIONAL PARK

Gold Coast: Lamington National Park is a pristine and picturesque national park located in the Gold Coast Hinterland of Queensland, Australia. It is renowned for its lush rainforests, breathtaking waterfalls, and diverse wildlife.

The park is part of the Gondwana Rainforests of Australia World Heritage Area, recognized for its outstanding universal value and ecological significance. Lamington National Park offers visitors a unique opportunity to explore and appreciate the natural wonders of the region.

One of the park's main attractions is its extensive network of walking tracks, which cater to a range of fitness levels and interests. The most iconic trail is the Border Track, a 21-kilometre (13-mile) track that follows the Queensland-New South Wales border. This trail offers panoramic views of the surrounding landscapes, including the valleys, mountains, and even the coastline on clear days.

In addition to the Border Track, Lamington National Park features other walking trails that lead to breathtaking lookout points and cascading waterfalls. Some notable waterfalls in the park include Elabana Falls, Chalahn Falls, and Moran Falls. Visitors can witness the power and beauty of these waterfalls while immersing themselves in the tranquil rainforest environment.

The park is also home to a remarkable array of wildlife, including rare and endangered species. Visitors may encounter colourful birds, such as the vibrant crimson rosella and the elusive Albert's lyrebird, known for its remarkable mimicry skills. Lamington National Park is also inhabited by a variety of reptiles, amphibians, and marsupials, including the iconic pademelons and red-necked wallabies.

For those interested in overnight stays, Lamington National Park offers several accommodation options, including the historic O'Reilly's Rainforest Retreat and various camping grounds. These accommodations allow visitors to fully immerse themselves in the park's natural beauty and experience the peacefulness of the rainforest after day-trippers have left.

Overall, Lamington National Park is a must-visit destination for nature lovers and outdoor enthusiasts. Its pristine rainforests, stunning waterfalls, and abundant wildlife make it a paradise for hikers, birdwatchers, and those seeking a tranquil retreat in the heart of nature.

COOLANGATTA AND TWEED COAST

Gold Coast: Coolangatta and Tweed Coast are two neighbouring coastal regions located at the southernmost end of the Gold Coast, straddling the border between Queensland and New South Wales in Australia. Here's a detailed overview of each area:

Coolangatta:
Coolangatta is a laid-back coastal suburb known for its beautiful beaches and relaxed atmosphere. Coolangatta Beach, the main attraction, offers pristine sands and excellent surfing conditions, making it popular among surfers and beach lovers. The area also features iconic headland Point Danger, which offers panoramic views of the ocean and the coastline. Point Danger is home to the

Captain Cook Memorial Lighthouse, a historical landmark paying homage to Captain James Cook's arrival in Queensland. Coolangatta's beachfront is lined with vibrant cafes, restaurants, and shops, providing a lively atmosphere for visitors to enjoy.

Tweed Coast:
The Tweed Coast is a picturesque stretch of coastline that extends into New South Wales, adjacent to Coolangatta. It is known for its natural beauty, pristine beaches, and tranquil ambiance. The region offers a variety of outdoor activities, including swimming, fishing, and beach walks. The Tweed River, a scenic waterway that winds through the area, provides opportunities for boating, kayaking, and fishing. The town of Kingscliff, located on the Tweed Coast, is a popular destination with its charming coastal village atmosphere, trendy cafes, and restaurants. The Tweed Coast also hosts annual events and festivals that showcase the region's culture and active lifestyle.

Both Coolangatta and the Tweed Coast offer a mix of relaxation, natural beauty, and coastal charm.

Visitors can enjoy the laid-back beach culture, indulge in water activities, explore the scenic surroundings, and immerse themselves in the welcoming coastal communities. Whether you seek a peaceful beachside retreat or an active seaside adventure, Coolangatta and the Tweed Coast provide a refreshing and rejuvenating experience for all.

SUNSHINE COAST

NOOSA HEADS AND NOOSA NATIONAL PARK

The Sunshine Coast is a picturesque region in Queensland, Australia, renowned for its stunning beaches and natural beauty. Noosa Heads and Noosa National Park are two of its prominent attractions. Here's a detailed yet concise overview:

Noosa Heads:
- Located at the northern end of the Sunshine Coast, Noosa Heads is a charming coastal town.
- It boasts pristine beaches, including the popular Main Beach and the renowned surfing spot, First Point.
- Noosa Heads offers a vibrant atmosphere with upscale boutiques, restaurants, and cafes lining the iconic Hastings Street.
- The town provides easy access to the Noosa River, where visitors can enjoy river cruises, fishing, and various water sports.

- The Noosa National Park is situated adjacent to Noosa Heads, offering a stunning natural backdrop for outdoor activities.

Noosa National Park:
- Noosa National Park is an expansive protected area situated east of Noosa Heads.
- Encompassing approximately 4,000 hectares, it showcases diverse ecosystems like coastal heathlands, rocky headlands, and eucalypt forests.
- The park features an extensive network of walking tracks suitable for different fitness levels, ranging from leisurely strolls to challenging hikes.
- The Coastal Track is a notable highlight, offering breathtaking coastal vistas and opportunities to spot wildlife like koalas, dolphins, and various bird species.
- Several picturesque beaches are nestled within the park, including Tea Tree Bay, Granite Bay, and Alexandria Bay, perfect for swimming, snorkelling, and enjoying picnics.
- Visitors can explore the enchanting Fairy Pools, natural tidal pools that provide a refreshing swimming experience.

Noosa Heads and Noosa National Park together provide a delightful blend of coastal charm, outdoor adventures, and natural wonders. Whether it's enjoying the beaches, indulging in gourmet delights, or immersing oneself in the park's scenic beauty, they offer an unforgettable experience on the Sunshine Coast.

AUSTRALIA ZOO

Australia Zoo is a world-renowned wildlife conservation facility located on the Sunshine Coast in Queensland, Australia. Here's a detailed and concise overview:

Australia Zoo:
- Founded by the late Steve Irwin, known as the "Crocodile Hunter," and his family, Australia Zoo is a major tourist attraction and a leading wildlife conservation centre.
- It is situated in Beerwah, approximately 80 kilometres north of Brisbane, making it easily accessible from the Sunshine Coast.

- The zoo spans over 100 acres and is home to a wide variety of Australian and international wildlife species.
- Visitors can observe and learn about animals such as kangaroos, koalas, crocodiles, snakes, birds, and big cats, among many others.
- The zoo offers various interactive experiences and shows, including crocodile feeding demonstrations, wildlife encounters, and educational talks.
- It focuses on promoting conservation and wildlife protection, with initiatives aimed at raising awareness about threatened species and supporting wildlife conservation projects.
- Australia Zoo has a strong emphasis on animal welfare and provides state-of-the-art enclosures and habitats that prioritise the well-being of the animals.
- The zoo offers a range of amenities and facilities, including restaurants, cafes, picnic areas, and a gift shop where visitors can find a variety of wildlife-themed merchandise.

Australia Zoo is not only a popular tourist destination but also an important hub for wildlife conservation efforts. With its unique animal encounters and educational programs, it provides an immersive and informative experience for visitors, while actively contributing to the preservation of Australia's diverse wildlife.

GLASS HOUSE MOUNTAINS

The Glass House Mountains are a prominent natural landmark located on the Sunshine Coast in Queensland, Australia. Here's a detailed and concise overview:

Glass House Mountains:
- The Glass House Mountains are a group of volcanic peaks situated about 70 kilometres north of Brisbane, on the Sunshine Coast.
- The mountains are named after their distinctive appearance, resembling glass furnaces used by early European settlers.
- They hold great cultural and spiritual significance to the traditional owners of the land, the Gubbi Gubbi people.

- The mountains are made up of 11 prominent peaks, including Mount Beerwah, Mount Tibrogargan, and Mount Coonowrin, among others.
- Each peak offers unique rock formations, stunning panoramic views, and opportunities for hiking and rock climbing.
- The Glass House Mountains are part of the Glass House Mountains National Park, which spans over 6,000 hectares and provides a range of recreational activities.
- The park offers several well-maintained walking tracks catering to different fitness levels, allowing visitors to explore the diverse flora and fauna of the area.
- Rock climbing enthusiasts can challenge themselves on the steep cliffs and challenging routes of the mountains.
- The region surrounding the Glass House Mountains is also known for its rich agricultural land, with fruit farms, wineries, and charming rural towns to explore.

The Glass House Mountains are a natural wonder on the Sunshine Coast, attracting visitors with their unique beauty, recreational opportunities, and cultural significance. Whether it's hiking to enjoy breathtaking views or immersing in the rich history of the region, the Glass House Mountains offer a memorable experience for nature lovers and outdoor enthusiasts.

MOOLOOLABA BEACH

Mooloolaba Beach is a stunning coastal destination located on the Sunshine Coast in Queensland, Australia. Here's a detailed and concise overview:

Mooloolaba Beach:
- Mooloolaba Beach is a popular and award-winning beach situated in the vibrant coastal town of Mooloolaba on the Sunshine Coast.
- It is known for its pristine white sand, clear turquoise waters, and a relaxed beachside atmosphere.
- Mooloolaba Beach offers a range of activities for visitors, including swimming, surfing, stand-up paddleboarding, and beach volleyball.

- The beach is patrolled by lifeguards, ensuring a safe swimming environment for visitors of all ages.
- Mooloolaba Spit, a picturesque headland at the northern end of the beach, provides a calm estuary where visitors can enjoy fishing, boating, and water sports.
- The Esplanade runs parallel to the beach and offers an array of waterfront dining options, cafes, boutique shops, and accommodations.
- Underwater World Sea Life Aquarium, located near Mooloolaba Beach, provides a chance to explore marine life through interactive exhibits and encounters.
- The beach hosts various events and festivals throughout the year, attracting both locals and tourists.
- Mooloolaba Beach is renowned for its stunning sunrises and sunsets, providing breathtaking views and photographic opportunities.

Mooloolaba Beach is a must-visit destination on the Sunshine Coast, offering a perfect blend of natural beauty, recreational activities, and a vibrant coastal atmosphere. Whether it's enjoying the beach, exploring the nearby attractions, or indulging in delicious cuisine, Mooloolaba Beach provides a memorable experience for beach lovers and holidaymakers.

FRASER ISLAND

Fraser Island, located on the Sunshine Coast of Queensland, Australia, is a world-renowned natural wonder and the largest sand island in the world. Here's a detailed and concise overview:

Fraser Island:
- Fraser Island is a UNESCO World Heritage Site and is known for its unique ecosystem, stunning landscapes, and diverse wildlife.
- It stretches over 123 kilometres in length and covers an area of approximately 184,000 hectares.
- The island is composed primarily of sand dunes and features ancient rainforests, crystal-clear freshwater lakes, expansive sandy beaches, and towering sand cliffs.

- It is home to a wide range of wildlife, including dingoes (native wild dogs), wallabies, echidnas, and various bird species.
- Fraser Island's most famous attraction is Lake McKenzie, a pristine freshwater lake with incredibly clear waters and white silica sand beaches.
- The island offers numerous natural wonders, such as the Champagne Pools, a unique formation of rock pools filled by crashing ocean waves, and the iconic Maheno Shipwreck, a rusted wreck on the beach.
- Visitors can explore Fraser Island by 4x4 vehicles, join guided tours, or embark on multi-day hikes to fully experience its beauty and natural wonders.
- The island provides opportunities for swimming, fishing, snorkelling, kayaking, and camping amidst breathtaking natural surroundings.
- It is important to note that due to its fragile ecosystem, visitors are encouraged to follow responsible tourism practices and respect the island's environment.

Fraser Island is a must-visit destination on the Sunshine Coast, offering a truly unique and unforgettable experience in a natural paradise. Its diverse landscapes, pristine lakes, and abundant wildlife make it a haven for nature lovers and outdoor enthusiasts.

WHITSUNDAY ISLANDS AND GREAT BARRIER REEF

Whitsunday Islands:
The Whitsunday Islands are a group of 74 islands located off the coast of Queensland, Australia. They are renowned for their stunning natural beauty, including pristine beaches, crystal-clear waters, and vibrant coral reefs. Some of the popular islands in the group include Hamilton Island, Hayman Island, and Whitsunday Island. The highlight of the Whitsundays is Whitehaven Beach, known for its pure white silica sand and breathtaking scenery. Visitors can engage in activities such as snorkelling, scuba diving, sailing, and hiking, while enjoying the tropical paradise offered by the islands.

Great Barrier Reef:
The Great Barrier Reef is the world's largest coral reef system, stretching over 2,300 kilometres

along the northeast coast of Queensland. It is a UNESCO World Heritage site and a global treasure of marine biodiversity. The reef is home to a rich and diverse ecosystem, including vibrant corals, tropical fish, turtles, dolphins, and more. Snorkelling, scuba diving, and boat tours are popular ways to explore the reef's incredible underwater world. The Whitsunday Islands are located within the Great Barrier Reef Marine Park, providing convenient access to this natural wonder. The combination of the Whitsunday Islands and the Great Barrier Reef offers visitors an unforgettable experience of stunning landscapes and unique marine life.

AIRLIE BEACH

Airlie Beach is a popular coastal town located in Queensland, Australia. Here's some detailed yet concise information about Airlie Beach:

Location and Accessibility:
Airlie Beach is situated on the east coast of Queensland, near the Great Barrier Reef. It is a

gateway to the Whitsunday Islands, making it a convenient starting point for exploring this tropical paradise. The town is easily accessible by road, with the Bruce Highway connecting it to major cities like Brisbane and Cairns. The Whitsunday Coast Airport, located about 40 minutes away, offers domestic flights for those travelling from further distances.

Vibrant Atmosphere:
Airlie Beach has a lively and laid-back atmosphere, attracting tourists from around the world. The town offers a range of accommodations, from budget hostels to luxury resorts, along with a variety of restaurants, bars, and shops. The main street, Shute Harbour Road, is bustling with activity and offers a vibrant nightlife scene.

Great Barrier Reef and Whitsunday Islands:
Airlie Beach serves as a launching point for exploring the Great Barrier Reef and the Whitsunday Islands. Numerous tour operators offer day trips and multi-day sailing adventures to these stunning destinations. Visitors can experience snorkelling, scuba diving, and scenic

cruises to witness the beauty of the Great Barrier Reef Marine Park and its vibrant coral reefs. The Whitsunday Islands, including iconic spots like Whitehaven Beach, are easily accessible from Airlie Beach and offer breathtaking scenery and outdoor activities.

Activities and Adventure:
In addition to reef and island exploration, Airlie Beach offers a range of activities for adventure enthusiasts. Visitors can go hiking in the Conway National Park, take scenic flights or helicopter tours over the reef and islands, and enjoy water sports such as jet skiing, paddleboarding, and kayaking. The town also serves as a hub for backpackers and offers backpacker-friendly accommodations and social events.

Airlie Beach is a vibrant coastal town that provides a perfect blend of relaxation, adventure, and natural beauty. With its convenient location and a wide array of activities and amenities, it is a popular destination for both international and domestic travellers looking to experience the wonders of the Great Barrier Reef and the Whitsunday Islands.

WHITEHAVEN BEACH

Whitehaven Beach is a world-renowned beach located on Whitsunday Island, the largest of the Whitsunday Islands in Queensland, Australia. Here's some detailed yet concise information about Whitehaven Beach:

Location and Features:
Whitehaven Beach is situated in the heart of the Great Barrier Reef, off the coast of Queensland. It stretches over seven kilometres along the eastern side of Whitsunday Island. The beach is famous for its powdery white silica sand, which is incredibly fine and doesn't retain heat, making it comfortable to walk on even on hot days. The pristine turquoise waters of the Coral Sea further enhance the beach's allure.

Pure Silica Sand and Unique Features:

Whitehaven Beach is renowned for its unique silica sand, which consists almost entirely of pure silica. The sand is incredibly fine and has a remarkably bright, white appearance. It is often compared to powdered sugar or talcum powder. Visitors are often captivated by the striking contrast between the vibrant blue hues of the ocean and the brilliant white sand. The beach's beauty is further accentuated by the surrounding lush greenery and rocky headlands.

Hill Inlet:
One of the most striking features of Whitehaven Beach is Hill Inlet, a stunning swirling inlet located at the northern end of the beach. As the tide shifts, the mix of sand and water creates mesmerising patterns of vibrant colours, ranging from azure to emerald. The view from the lookout point above Hill Inlet provides a breathtaking panorama of this natural phenomenon and is a popular spot for photography.

Activities and Accessibility:
Whitehaven Beach offers various activities for visitors to enjoy. Swimming and sunbathing on the

pristine shores are popular pastimes, while the clear waters provide excellent opportunities for snorkelling to discover the nearby coral reefs and marine life. Visitors can also take leisurely walks along the beach, explore the nearby Whitsunday Islands, or embark on boat tours that provide access to different parts of the beach and the surrounding reef.

Accessibility to Whitehaven Beach is primarily through Airlie Beach, which serves as a launching point for tours and cruises. Boats and seaplanes transport visitors to the beach, allowing them to experience its beauty firsthand.

Whitehaven Beach's unparalleled natural beauty, pure silica sand, and striking scenery make it a must-visit destination for those exploring the Whitsunday Islands and the Great Barrier Reef. It is a place of tranquillity and natural wonder that captivates visitors from around the world.

GREAT BARRIER REEF MARINE PARK

Great Barrier Reef Marine Park is a vast protected area located off the coast of Queensland, Australia. It is one of the most iconic and ecologically significant marine parks in the world. Here's some detailed yet concise information about the Great Barrier Reef Marine Park:

Size and Importance:
The Great Barrier Reef Marine Park spans an area of approximately 344,400 square kilometres, making it the largest coral reef system on the planet. It is a UNESCO World Heritage site and a globally recognized symbol of natural beauty and biodiversity. The reef plays a crucial role in supporting marine life, acting as a habitat for thousands of species, including corals, fish, turtles, dolphins, and countless other forms of marine plants and animals.

Biodiversity and Ecosystems:

The marine park is renowned for its unparalleled biodiversity. It is estimated to be home to over 1,500 species of fish, 600 species of coral, and a vast array of other marine organisms. The reef's complex ecosystems, including coral reefs, seagrass beds, mangrove forests, and sandy cays, provide a diverse range of habitats for marine life to thrive. It is considered a hotspot of biological diversity and a vital breeding ground for many species.

Conservation and Protection:
The Great Barrier Reef Marine Park is rigorously managed and protected to ensure its long-term survival. The park has designated zones that allow for different activities while safeguarding the reef's health. Certain areas are strictly protected as no-take zones, where fishing and collection of marine life are prohibited. Sustainable tourism practices and strict regulations are in place to minimise human impact and preserve the fragile ecosystem.

Threats and Conservation Efforts:

The Great Barrier Reef faces several significant threats, including climate change, ocean acidification, pollution, overfishing, and coastal development. These factors have resulted in coral bleaching events and a decline in overall reef health. Extensive conservation efforts are being undertaken to mitigate these threats, including initiatives to reduce greenhouse gas emissions, improve water quality, and enhance the reef's resilience. Collaboration between government agencies, scientists, conservation organisations, and local communities is crucial in protecting and restoring the reef's ecosystem.

Visitor Experiences:
The marine park offers a range of incredible experiences for visitors. Snorkelling and scuba diving allow people to explore the vibrant coral reefs and encounter the reef's diverse marine life up close. Boat tours, cruises, and helicopter flights provide panoramic views of the reef's breathtaking beauty. Educational centres and interpretive exhibits offer insights into the reef's ecology, conservation efforts, and indigenous cultural connections to the region. Visitors are encouraged

to practise responsible tourism, follow guidelines, and support initiatives that contribute to the long-term protection of the Great Barrier Reef Marine Park.

HAMILTON ISLAND

Hamilton Island is a picturesque island located in the Whitsunday Islands group off the coast of Queensland, Australia. Here's some detailed yet concise information about Hamilton Island:

Location and Accessibility:
Hamilton Island is nestled within the Whitsunday Islands, making it easily accessible by air and sea. The island has its own airport, the Great Barrier Reef Airport, which offers direct flights from major Australian cities such as Sydney, Melbourne, and Brisbane. Alternatively, visitors can take a ferry or yacht from Airlie Beach, which is the main gateway to the Whitsunday Islands.

Accommodations and Amenities:

Hamilton Island is known for its world-class accommodations and amenities. The island offers a range of options, from luxury resorts to self-contained apartments, providing something for every traveller's taste and budget. The island's marina precinct features shops, restaurants, and cafes, where visitors can indulge in shopping and dining experiences. The island also has a golf course, a wildlife park, and a variety of water sports facilities.

Natural Beauty and Outdoor Activities:
Hamilton Island is surrounded by the crystal-clear waters of the Great Barrier Reef, offering breathtaking views and access to a diverse underwater world. Snorkelling and diving are popular activities, allowing visitors to explore the vibrant coral reefs and encounter marine life such as colourful fish, turtles, and even dolphins. The island also boasts beautiful hiking trails that lead to scenic lookouts, providing panoramic views of the island and the surrounding Whitsunday Islands.

Whitehaven Beach and Great Barrier Reef:

Hamilton Island serves as a starting point for visiting nearby attractions, such as Whitehaven Beach and the Great Barrier Reef. Visitors can embark on day trips or overnight sailing adventures to experience the world-famous Whitehaven Beach with its pristine white silica sand and turquoise waters. The island's location within the heart of the Great Barrier Reef also allows for easy access to snorkelling and diving spots, ensuring unforgettable experiences exploring the reef's diverse ecosystems.

Hamilton Island is a tropical paradise that offers a combination of natural beauty, luxury accommodations, and a wide range of activities. Its accessibility, stunning surroundings, and proximity to iconic attractions make it a popular destination for those seeking an unforgettable island getaway in Queensland.

WHITSUNDAY ISLANDS

NATIONAL PARK

Whitsunday Islands National Park is a protected area encompassing several islands within the Whitsunday Islands group off the coast of Queensland, Australia. Here's some detailed yet concise information about Whitsunday Islands National Park:

Location and Size:
Whitsunday Islands National Park is located in the heart of the Great Barrier Reef, off the coast of Queensland. It covers a significant portion of the Whitsunday Islands, which consist of 74 islands, including popular ones like Whitsunday Island, Hook Island, and Hayman Island. The park spans approximately 27,508 hectares, preserving the islands' unique ecosystems and natural beauty.

Biodiversity and Marine Life:
The national park is renowned for its rich biodiversity, both on land and underwater. The islands are home to a diverse range of flora and

fauna, including unique plant species, nesting seabirds, and diverse marine life. The coral reefs surrounding the islands are part of the Great Barrier Reef Marine Park and provide habitats for vibrant corals, tropical fish, turtles, and other marine creatures.

Outdoor Activities:
Whitsunday Islands National Park offers various recreational activities for visitors to enjoy. Popular activities include hiking, camping, and wildlife spotting on the islands. The park features several walking tracks, ranging from short walks to longer hikes, providing opportunities to explore the islands' lush rainforests, scenic viewpoints, and secluded beaches. Snorkelling and diving in the park's pristine waters allow visitors to discover the stunning coral reefs and marine life.

Cultural Heritage:
The Whitsunday Islands hold significant cultural and historical value for the Indigenous traditional owners, the Ngaro people. The islands have a rich Aboriginal and European history, with evidence of Indigenous occupation dating back thousands of

years. Visitors can learn about the cultural heritage of the area through interpretive signs and cultural tours, respecting the cultural sensitivities and importance of the land to the traditional custodians.

Conservation and Management:
Whitsunday Islands National Park is managed by Queensland Parks and Wildlife Service to protect its natural and cultural values. Conservation efforts focus on preserving the islands' ecosystems, managing visitor impacts, and ensuring sustainable tourism practices. The park's diverse environments are fragile and require ongoing protection to maintain their ecological integrity and ensure future generations can enjoy their beauty.

Whitsunday Islands National Park is a captivating destination offering a unique blend of natural beauty, outdoor activities, and cultural significance. With its stunning landscapes, abundant marine life, and opportunities for exploration, the park provides a memorable experience for visitors seeking to immerse themselves in the wonders of the Whitsunday Islands.

CAIRNS AND TROPICAL NORTH QUEENSLAND

EXPLORING CAIRNS

Exploring Cairns in Queensland offers a wealth of exciting experiences and attractions. Here's a detailed yet concise overview of what you can expect when exploring Cairns:

1. Great Barrier Reef: Cairns is the gateway to the Great Barrier Reef, one of the world's most magnificent natural wonders. You can embark on snorkelling or scuba diving tours to witness the vibrant coral reefs, colourful marine life, and even spot turtles, reef sharks, and dolphins.

2. Cairns Esplanade: The Cairns Esplanade is a lively waterfront promenade offering a range of activities. Take a dip in the lagoon, relax in the shaded parklands, enjoy a barbecue, or explore the Night Markets featuring local crafts, food, and live entertainment.

3. Kuranda Village: Visit the picturesque village of Kuranda, nestled in the rainforest near Cairns. Enjoy a scenic journey on the Kuranda Scenic Railway or the Skyrail Rainforest Cableway, browse through the vibrant markets, visit wildlife sanctuaries, and explore stunning walking trails.

4. Daintree Rainforest: Venture north of Cairns to discover the ancient Daintree Rainforest, a UNESCO World Heritage site. Take guided walks through lush greenery, cruise along the Daintree River to spot crocodiles, and immerse yourself in the rich biodiversity and cultural heritage of this remarkable ecosystem.

5. Atherton Tablelands: Head inland from Cairns to the Atherton Tablelands, a region of breathtaking landscapes and charming rural towns. Explore waterfalls such as Millaa Millaa Falls and Josephine Falls, discover the stunning crater lakes, and indulge in local produce, including tropical fruits and dairy products.

6. Port Douglas: Located just north of Cairns, Port Douglas offers a laid-back coastal experience. Relax on the famous Four Mile Beach, visit the bustling Macrossan Street lined with shops and restaurants, and enjoy a range of water activities, including snorkelling, sailing, and fishing.

7. Indigenous Experiences: Learn about the rich Indigenous culture of the region through various tours and activities. Visit Tjapukai Aboriginal Cultural Park to experience traditional dance performances and interactive exhibits, or join a guided tour to explore ancient rock art sites and gain insights into the local Aboriginal and Torres Strait Islander communities.

8. Adventure Activities: Cairns is a hub for adrenaline-pumping adventures. Take a leap with bungee jumping or skydiving, navigate the rapids while white-water rafting on the Tully or Barron River, or soar above the rainforest canopy on a thrilling ziplining tour.

9. Cairns Botanic Gardens: Spend a peaceful day at the Cairns Botanic Gardens, home to a vast

collection of tropical plants and flowers. Explore themed gardens, including the Aboriginal Plant Use Garden, Rainforest Boardwalk, and Flecker Gardens showcasing native flora.

10. Fitzroy Island: Embark on a day trip to Fitzroy Island, located a short boat ride from Cairns. Relax on the pristine beaches, hike through lush rainforest trails, or snorkel the fringing coral reefs teeming with marine life.

Exploring Cairns in Queensland promises a memorable blend of natural wonders, cultural experiences, and thrilling adventures, making it an ideal destination for diverse interests and preferences.

GREAT BARRIER REEF SNORKELLING AND DIVING

Great Barrier Reef Snorkeling and Diving in Queensland offer unparalleled opportunities to explore the world's largest coral reef system.

Here's a detailed yet concise overview of what you can expect when snorkelling or diving in the Great Barrier Reef:

1. Location: The Great Barrier Reef is located off the coast of Queensland, stretching over 2,300 kilometres (1,400 miles). Cairns and Port Douglas are popular starting points for reef adventures.

2. Coral Reefs: The Great Barrier Reef is composed of thousands of individual reefs and hundreds of islands, home to a diverse array of coral species. Snorkelers and divers can explore vibrant coral gardens, bommies (coral outcrops), and reef walls.

3. Marine Life: The reef supports a staggering variety of marine life. Snorkelers and divers can encounter colourful fish, including clownfish (Nemo), parrotfish, and butterflyfish. Keep an eye out for larger species like turtles, reef sharks, rays, and even dolphins.

4. Snorkelling: Snorkelling is a popular activity for exploring the reef's shallow areas. With a mask, snorkel, and fins, you can float at the surface and

observe the underwater world. Many snorkelling tours provide flotation devices and expert guides to ensure a safe and enjoyable experience.

5. Scuba Diving: Scuba diving allows you to explore the reef at greater depths and witness its full splendour. Certified divers can choose from a variety of dive sites catering to different skill levels, from beginner-friendly sites with gentle currents to advanced locations with thrilling wall dives or famous sites like the Cod Hole or Osprey Reef.

6. Dive Certification: If you're not a certified diver, you can obtain an Open Water certification through a multi-day course. It includes theory, pool training, and open water dives, enabling you to explore the reef's wonders with confidence.

7. Liveaboard Trips: For an immersive experience, consider a liveaboard trip where you stay on a boat for multiple days. Liveaboards offer extended dive opportunities, including night dives, and access to remote areas of the reef.

8. Snorkeling and Diving Tours: Numerous operators in Cairns and Port Douglas offer snorkelling and diving tours to the Great Barrier Reef. These tours provide transportation, equipment, and professional guides who offer insights about the reef's ecology and ensure safety.

9. Conservation and Sustainability: The Great Barrier Reef faces challenges from climate change and human impacts. Visitors are encouraged to choose operators committed to responsible reef practices and adhere to guidelines such as reef-safe sunscreen usage and not touching or damaging the delicate coral.

10. Accessibility: Snorkelling and introductory diving experiences are available for individuals of various ages and fitness levels. Specialised tours cater to non-swimmers or those with limited mobility, providing platforms and guided experiences for a memorable reef encounter.

Snorkelling and diving in the Great Barrier Reef offer a once-in-a-lifetime opportunity to immerse yourself in an underwater paradise teeming with life. Whether you're a beginner or an experienced diver, exploring this natural wonder will leave you with unforgettable memories of its breathtaking beauty.

DAINTREE RAINFOREST AND CAPE TRIBULATION

Daintree Rainforest and Cape Tribulation in Queensland offer a captivating combination of ancient rainforest, pristine beaches, and unique wildlife. Here's a detailed yet concise overview of these two remarkable destinations:

1. Daintree Rainforest: The Daintree Rainforest is one of the oldest rainforests in the world and a UNESCO World Heritage site. Located north of Cairns, it spans over 1,200 square kilometres (460 square miles) and is known for its incredible biodiversity and lush greenery.

2. Ancient Ecosystem: The Daintree Rainforest is estimated to be over 180 million years old,

predating even the Amazon rainforest. It is home to a diverse range of plant and animal species, including rare and endemic flora and fauna.

3. Boardwalks and Trails: Explore the rainforest through a network of boardwalks and walking trails. The Marrdja Botanical Walk and Jindalba Boardwalk are popular choices, allowing visitors to immerse themselves in the rainforest's tranquil ambiance while learning about its unique ecosystem.

4. Wildlife Spotting: The Daintree Rainforest is teeming with wildlife. Keep an eye out for the elusive cassowary, a large flightless bird found only in this region. You may also spot tree kangaroos, possums, colourful birds like the paradise kingfisher, and a variety of reptiles and insects.

5. Daintree River: Take a cruise along the Daintree River for a chance to spot estuarine crocodiles in their natural habitat. Knowledgeable guides provide fascinating insights into the ecosystem and wildlife behaviour.

6. Mossman Gorge: Adjacent to the Daintree Rainforest, Mossman Gorge is a must-visit destination. Embark on a guided walk through the gorge, swim in its crystal-clear waters, and learn about the Indigenous culture and traditions associated with the area.

7. Cape Tribulation: Located within the Daintree Rainforest, Cape Tribulation is a picturesque coastal area where the rainforest meets the Great Barrier Reef. It offers stunning white-sand beaches, turquoise waters, and a sense of untouched beauty.

8. Beaches and Swimming Holes: Cape Tribulation boasts beautiful beaches such as Myall Beach and Coconut Beach. Additionally, you can find refreshing swimming holes along the creeks, including Emmagen Creek and Mason's Swimming Hole.

9. Adventure Activities: Cape Tribulation provides opportunities for adventure enthusiasts. Experience jungle surfing, where you glide

through the rainforest canopy on ziplines, or embark on guided night walks to discover the nocturnal creatures that come alive in the rainforest.

10. Eco-Lodges and Resorts: Stay at one of the eco-lodges or resorts in the area to fully immerse yourself in the rainforest experience. These accommodations often blend seamlessly with nature and offer a range of amenities and guided tours to enhance your stay.

Daintree Rainforest and Cape Tribulation offer a unique opportunity to witness the wonders of an ancient rainforest and bask in the beauty of pristine beaches. Whether you're seeking adventure, tranquillity, or a deeper connection with nature, these destinations will leave you enchanted by their natural splendour.

KURANDA SCENIC RAILWAY AND SKYRAIL

The Kuranda Scenic Railway and Skyrail Rainforest Cableway are two popular attractions in Queensland that offer stunning views and immersive experiences in the rainforest. Here's a detailed yet concise overview of each:

1. Kuranda Scenic Railway: The Kuranda Scenic Railway is a historic train journey that takes you through the picturesque rainforest from Cairns to the village of Kuranda. This scenic railway winds its way through lush mountains, offering panoramic views of waterfalls, gorges, and dense vegetation. The journey provides insights into the region's history and showcases the beauty of the surrounding landscape.

2. Train Experience: The Kuranda Scenic Railway features heritage-style carriages with comfortable seating, large windows, and historical charm. As you travel along the railway, an informative commentary provides fascinating facts about the

region's geography, flora, fauna, and Aboriginal history. The journey includes passing through tunnels, crossing bridges, and making stops at scenic viewpoints.

3. Barron Gorge: One of the highlights of the Kuranda Scenic Railway is the Barron Gorge, a majestic natural wonder. As the train traverses the gorge, you'll be treated to breathtaking views of the steep cliffs and the cascading Barron Falls. The train slows down at viewpoints, allowing ample time to admire and capture photos of this impressive sight.

4. Kuranda Village: The Kuranda Scenic Railway journey concludes in the village of Kuranda. Known for its vibrant arts and crafts scene, Kuranda offers a range of shops, galleries, and local markets where you can browse unique handmade goods and souvenirs. You can also explore the village's lush gardens, visit wildlife attractions, or enjoy a meal at one of the local cafes or restaurants.

5. Skyrail Rainforest Cableway: The Skyrail Rainforest Cableway is a unique cable car experience that takes you on an aerial journey above the rainforest canopy. The cableway spans from Kuranda to the town of Smithfield near Cairns, offering breathtaking views of the lush rainforest, Barron Gorge, and Coral Sea.

6. Cable Car Experience: Skyrail features comfortable gondola cabins that provide 360-degree views of the surrounding landscape. The cableway stops at two rainforest stations, allowing you to disembark and explore the rainforest up close. At each station, you can follow elevated boardwalks, learn about the rainforest's flora and fauna through interpretive displays, and take in the tranquil beauty of the ancient forest.

7. Rainforest Interpretation: Skyrail offers an educational experience with informative displays and audio commentary available in multiple languages. Learn about the rainforest's biodiversity, ecological importance, and the cultural significance of the area to the Indigenous people.

8. Barron Falls Station: One of the highlights of the Skyrail experience is the Barron Falls Station, situated near the majestic Barron Falls. Here, you can disembark and take in the awe-inspiring views of the falls from a specially designed viewing platform. The sight and sound of the cascading water surrounded by lush greenery create a memorable experience.

9. Sustainable Tourism: Both the Kuranda Scenic Railway and Skyrail Rainforest Cableway are committed to sustainable tourism practices. They focus on preserving the rainforest, supporting local communities, and providing educational experiences to promote environmental awareness.

The Kuranda Scenic Railway and Skyrail Rainforest Cableway offer unique ways to experience the beauty of Queensland's rainforest. Whether you choose the historic train journey or the cable car adventure, both experiences provide unforgettable views and insights into this ancient and diverse ecosystem.

ATHERTON TABLELANDS

The Atherton Tablelands in Queensland is a breathtaking region located inland from Cairns. Here's a detailed yet concise overview of the Atherton Tablelands:

1. Location and Landscape: The Atherton Tablelands is a fertile plateau situated in the Great Dividing Range. It covers an expansive area of approximately 32,000 square kilometres (12,355 square miles) and offers diverse landscapes, including rolling hills, lush rainforest, volcanic craters, and cascading waterfalls.

2. Waterfalls: The region is renowned for its stunning waterfalls. Millaa Millaa Falls, Zillie Falls, and Ellinjaa Falls are just a few of the captivating cascades that can be found in the area. You can swim, picnic, or simply admire the beauty of these natural wonders.

3. Crater Lakes: The Atherton Tablelands is home to several picturesque crater lakes formed by ancient volcanic activity. Lake Barrine and Lake

Eacham are popular destinations where visitors can enjoy swimming, kayaking, or leisurely walks along the tranquil lakeside trails.

4. Wildlife and Nature: The region boasts abundant wildlife and biodiversity. Keep an eye out for unique species like the Lumholtz's tree-kangaroo, platypus, and colourful birds such as the Victoria's riflebird. Explore the numerous national parks and reserves to experience the rich natural beauty and encounter native flora and fauna.

5. Coffee and Plantations: The Atherton Tablelands is known for its fertile soil, making it ideal for agriculture. The region is dotted with coffee plantations, where you can learn about the coffee-making process, sample local brews, and enjoy scenic views of sprawling plantations.

6. Local Produce and Markets: The Atherton Tablelands is a food lover's paradise. Explore the local markets in towns like Yungaburra and Atherton, where you can indulge in fresh tropical fruits, artisan cheeses, homemade jams, and other delectable local produce.

7. Historic Towns: The region is home to charming historic towns that offer glimpses into the area's rich heritage. Yungaburra, Herberton, and Atherton are notable examples, featuring heritage-listed buildings, quaint streets, and museums that showcase the region's past.

8. Water Activities: The Atherton Tablelands provides opportunities for water-based activities. Lake Tinaroo, a man-made reservoir, offers fishing, boating, and camping experiences. Visitors can also enjoy swimming in the pristine waters of the many natural swimming holes and creeks.

9. Adventure Sports: The Atherton Tablelands caters to adventure enthusiasts with activities such as mountain biking, hiking, and hot air ballooning. Explore the extensive network of trails through the rainforest, challenge yourself on thrilling biking routes, or take to the skies for a breathtaking aerial view of the landscape.

10. Indigenous Culture: The Atherton Tablelands has a rich Indigenous heritage. Visitors can engage with the local Indigenous communities and learn about their cultural traditions, dreamtime stories, and connection to the land through guided tours and cultural experiences.

The Atherton Tablelands is a captivating region that offers a blend of natural wonders, cultural experiences, and culinary delights. Whether you seek adventure, relaxation, or a deeper connection with nature, this diverse region will leave you with lasting memories.

TOWNSVILLE, MAGNETIC ISLAND, AND NORTH QUEENSLAND

TOWNSVILLE CITY TOUR

The Townsville City Tour in Queensland offers visitors a glimpse into the vibrant history, natural beauty, and cultural attractions of this coastal city. Here is a detailed yet concise overview of what you can expect from a Townsville City Tour:

1. Introduction to Townsville:
The tour typically begins with an introduction to Townsville's history, highlighting its origins as a 19th-century port city and its growth into a modern urban centre. You'll learn about the indigenous heritage of the region and the European settlement that shaped the city.

2. Strand Esplanade:

One of the highlights of the tour is a visit to the Strand Esplanade, a picturesque waterfront promenade stretching for 2.2 kilometres. Here, you can enjoy stunning views of Magnetic Island and relax on the sandy beaches. The Strand also features recreational facilities, restaurants, cafes, and a water park, making it a popular spot for locals and visitors alike.

3. Castle Hill:

Next, you'll venture to Castle Hill, a prominent pink granite monolith that overlooks the city. A short drive or hike will take you to the summit, offering panoramic views of Townsville, its surrounding islands, and the Coral Sea. The hill is an iconic landmark and provides an ideal opportunity for memorable photos.

4. Cultural Attractions:

Townsville is rich in cultural attractions, and the tour may include visits to some of the key landmarks. The Museum of Tropical Queensland showcases the region's natural and cultural heritage, including the famous wreck of the HMS Pandora. The Perc Tucker Regional Gallery exhibits contemporary and indigenous artworks, while the Cultural Centre houses the North Queensland Opera and Ballet.

5. Reef HQ Great Barrier Reef Aquarium:
For those interested in marine life, a visit to Reef HQ is a must. As the world's largest living coral reef aquarium, it offers a unique opportunity to explore the wonders of the Great Barrier Reef without getting wet. You can observe various coral species, colourful fish, and other marine creatures while learning about conservation efforts.

6. Townsville CBD:
The tour might also take you through the Townsville Central Business District (CBD), where you can experience the city's lively atmosphere, explore local shops, and appreciate the mix of modern and heritage architecture. The CBD is home to various dining options, allowing you to savour local cuisine during your visit.

7. Optional Additions:
Depending on the specific tour package, there may be additional optional activities. These could

include a visit to the Billabong Sanctuary, where you can interact with Australian wildlife, or a ferry ride to Magnetic Island for a closer look at its beaches, walking trails, and wildlife.

Overall, the Townsville City Tour offers a diverse range of experiences, allowing you to appreciate the city's natural beauty, cultural heritage, and unique attractions. Whether you're interested in history, nature, or simply soaking up the local atmosphere, this tour provides a comprehensive introduction to Townsville, Queensland.

MAGNETIC ISLAND NATIONAL PARK

Magnetic Island National Park is a captivating nature reserve located just off the coast of Townsville in Queensland, Australia. Here is a detailed yet concise overview of this beautiful park:

1. Location and Access:

Magnetic Island National Park spans over 5,000 hectares and encompasses more than half of Magnetic Island itself. It is easily accessible via a short 20-minute ferry ride from Townsville.

2. Natural Beauty:
The national park is renowned for its stunning natural beauty, featuring a combination of rugged granite hills, pristine beaches, and dense eucalypt forests. It offers a diverse range of habitats, including rainforests, woodlands, and coastal environments.

3. Walking Tracks:
There are numerous walking tracks throughout the national park, catering to different fitness levels and interests. Some popular trails include the Forts Walk, which leads to the historic World War II fortifications and offers panoramic views, and the Nelly Bay to Arcadia trail, a scenic coastal walk passing through beautiful beaches.

4. Wildlife:
Magnetic Island National Park is home to a rich variety of wildlife. As you explore the park, you

may encounter koalas, wallabies, possums, and a wide array of bird species, including the island's iconic bright blue Ulysses butterfly.

5. Snorkeling and Diving:
The marine environment surrounding Magnetic Island is part of the Great Barrier Reef Marine Park. Visitors can enjoy snorkelling and diving in the clear waters to discover an underwater world teeming with colourful coral reefs and marine life, including turtles, tropical fish, and even reef sharks.

6. Picnic Areas and Beaches:
The national park offers several picnic areas with facilities for visitors to relax, have a meal, and enjoy the surroundings. The beaches on Magnetic Island, such as Horseshoe Bay and Alma Bay, provide opportunities for swimming, sunbathing, and water sports.

7. Cultural Heritage:
Magnetic Island has a rich cultural heritage, with evidence of Aboriginal occupation dating back thousands of years. The park's trails often pass by

significant cultural sites, and there are interpretive displays providing insights into the island's Indigenous history and connection to the land.

8. Conservation Efforts:
The national park plays an essential role in the conservation of Magnetic Island's unique ecosystems. Efforts are made to protect and preserve the island's flora and fauna, including ongoing initiatives to manage invasive species and maintain the park's ecological integrity.

Magnetic Island National Park offers a combination of natural wonders, recreational activities, and cultural significance. Whether you're seeking adventure, relaxation, or a deeper understanding of the region's heritage, a visit to this picturesque park is sure to leave a lasting impression.

THE STRAND AND CASTLE HILL

The Strand and Castle Hill are two popular attractions located in Townsville, Queensland. Here is a detailed yet concise overview of each:

1. The Strand:
The Strand is a vibrant and picturesque waterfront promenade in Townsville. Stretching for 2.2 kilometres, it offers stunning views of the Coral Sea and Magnetic Island. The Strand features a sandy beach, palm-lined pathways, and recreational facilities such as picnic areas, BBQ spots, playgrounds, and a water park. Visitors can enjoy swimming, sunbathing, cycling, and walking along the scenic promenade. The Strand also boasts a range of restaurants, cafes, and shops, making it a lively hub for locals and tourists alike. It's a perfect place to relax, soak up the sun, and enjoy the beauty of Townsville's coastline.

2. Castle Hill:
Castle Hill is an iconic pink granite monolith that dominates the Townsville skyline. Rising 286 metres above sea level, it offers panoramic views

of the city, Magnetic Island, and the surrounding region. Visitors can reach the summit of Castle Hill by car, bus, or on foot via a series of walking tracks. The popular Goat Track is a challenging trail that rewards hikers with breathtaking vistas along the way. At the top, there are lookout points, seating areas, and binoculars to admire the panoramic views. Castle Hill is not only a natural landmark but also a favourite spot for fitness enthusiasts who enjoy walking, jogging, and exercising while taking in the magnificent scenery.

Both the Strand and Castle Hill are iconic landmarks in Townsville, offering visitors a chance to appreciate the natural beauty and recreational opportunities that the region has to offer. Whether you're looking for a leisurely stroll along the waterfront or a challenging hike with rewarding views, these attractions provide an unforgettable experience in Queensland.

HINCHINBROOK ISLAND

Hinchinbrook Island is a pristine and picturesque island located on the northeastern coast of Queensland, Australia. Here is a detailed yet concise overview of Hinchinbrook Island:

1. Location and Access:
Hinchinbrook Island is situated within the Great Barrier Reef Marine Park, approximately halfway between Townsville and Cairns. It is the largest island national park in Australia, covering an area of about 393 square kilometres. Access to the island is by boat, with regular ferry services available from the mainland.

2. Natural Beauty and Biodiversity:
Hinchinbrook Island is renowned for its unspoiled natural beauty and diverse ecosystems. It features rugged mountains, lush rainforests, pristine beaches, and crystal-clear creeks. The island is home to an abundance of wildlife, including over 1,000 plant species, 33 mammal species, and a variety of reptiles and birdlife. It offers a unique

opportunity to immerse oneself in a truly untouched natural environment.

3. Thorsborne Trail:
The Thorsborne Trail is one of the main attractions on Hinchinbrook Island. It is a 32-kilometre long hiking trail that winds through the island's rainforest and along its coastline. The trail takes approximately 4-6 days to complete and offers breathtaking views, secluded beaches, and opportunities for swimming and fishing. Permits are required to hike the Thorsborne Trail, and it is recommended to book in advance due to limited availability.

4. Wildlife and Marine Life:
Hinchinbrook Island is a haven for wildlife enthusiasts and nature lovers. The island is home to a diverse range of animal species, including the elusive and endangered cassowaries, agile wallabies, and various reptiles such as pythons and skinks. The surrounding marine waters are teeming with marine life, making it an ideal spot for snorkelling, diving, and fishing. Visitors may

encounter turtles, dolphins, dugongs, and a myriad of colourful fish and coral.

5. Conservation and Protection:
Hinchinbrook Island is protected as a national park, ensuring the preservation of its unique ecosystems and wildlife. The island's remote location and limited human impact have contributed to its pristine condition. Visitors are encouraged to practise responsible tourism, respecting the environment and adhering to park regulations to help preserve the island's natural integrity.

Hinchinbrook Island offers a serene and untouched escape into nature, with its rugged landscapes, stunning beaches, and abundant wildlife. Whether you embark on the Thorsborne Trail or simply explore its natural wonders, a visit to Hinchinbrook Island is an unforgettable experience for those seeking a pristine and remote island adventure in Queensland.

PALUMA RANGE NATIONAL PARK

Paluma Range National Park is a scenic and biodiverse park located in Queensland, Australia. Here is a detailed yet concise overview of Paluma Range National Park:

1. Location and Access:
Paluma Range National Park is situated in the Great Dividing Range, approximately 90 kilometres north of Townsville. The park encompasses an area of around 55,000 hectares and is easily accessible by road via the Bruce Highway.

2. Rainforests and Waterfalls:
The park is characterised by its lush rainforests, pristine creeks, and cascading waterfalls. Visitors can explore a network of walking tracks that lead through the dense vegetation, providing opportunities to immerse themselves in the beauty of the natural surroundings. Popular waterfalls within the park include Jourama Falls, Crystal

Creek Falls, and Big Crystal Creek Falls, each offering breathtaking views and natural swimming holes.

3. Biodiversity:

Paluma Range National Park is renowned for its rich biodiversity. The park is home to an array of plant and animal species, including ancient ferns, towering trees, and a variety of wildlife. Birdwatchers will be delighted by the presence of numerous species, including the elusive southern cassowary. Other animals that can be encountered in the park include wallabies, possums, and echidnas.

4. Camping and Picnic Areas:

The park provides several camping and picnic areas, allowing visitors to relax and enjoy the natural surroundings. Big Crystal Creek, in particular, offers picnic facilities and a designated camping area where visitors can spend the night surrounded by the sounds of the rainforest. Camping permits are required and can be obtained in advance.

5. Lookout Points:
Paluma Range National Park features several lookout points that offer stunning panoramic views of the surrounding landscapes. McClelland's Lookout and Paluma Lookout provide vistas over the coastal plains and the Coral Sea, while Cloudy Creek Lookout provides a picturesque view of the Paluma Dam and the rainforest below.

6. Paluma Village:
Nestled within the national park is Paluma Village, a small mountain hamlet that serves as a gateway to the park's attractions. The village offers accommodation options, cafes, and a visitor centre providing information about the park's trails, flora, and fauna.

Paluma Range National Park is a haven for nature enthusiasts, offering a blend of lush rainforests, refreshing waterfalls, and abundant wildlife. Whether you're seeking a peaceful picnic spot, an exhilarating hike, or a chance to immerse yourself in nature, this park provides a captivating experience in the heart of Queensland.

FRASER COAST AND BUNDABERG

HERVEY BAY

Hervey Bay is a coastal city located in Queensland, Australia. It is situated approximately 290 kilometres (180 miles) north of the state capital, Brisbane. Here are some key points about Hervey Bay:

1. Location: Hervey Bay is situated on the eastern coast of Australia, along the shores of the Coral Sea. It is part of the Fraser Coast region and is bordered by the Great Sandy Strait to the east.

2. Fraser Island: One of the main attractions of Hervey Bay is its close proximity to Fraser Island, the largest sand island in the world. The island is renowned for its stunning natural beauty, including pristine beaches, crystal-clear lakes, and ancient rainforests.

3. Whale Watching: Hervey Bay is considered one of the best places in the world for whale watching. Each year, between July and November, humpback whales migrate from Antarctica to the warmer waters of Hervey Bay to rest and play. Visitors can take boat tours to witness these magnificent creatures up close.

4. The Esplanade: Hervey Bay's Esplanade is a popular waterfront area that stretches along the bay. It features a scenic pathway for walking and cycling, as well as picnic spots, BBQ areas, and a variety of restaurants, cafes, and shops. The Esplanade is a great place to relax and enjoy the coastal atmosphere.

5. Beaches: Hervey Bay is blessed with beautiful sandy beaches. Torquay Beach, Scarness Beach, and Urangan Beach are some of the well-known spots for swimming, sunbathing, and water sports. The calm waters of the bay make it a safe and family-friendly destination.

6. Urangan Pier: The Urangan Pier is an iconic landmark in Hervey Bay. It stretches out 868

metres (2,848 feet) into the bay and offers panoramic views of the surrounding area. The pier is a popular spot for fishing and also serves as a departure point for boat tours to Fraser Island.

7. Fishing and Water Activities: Hervey Bay is a haven for fishing enthusiasts. The region offers excellent fishing opportunities, both from the shore and on chartered fishing boats. In addition, water activities such as jet skiing, kayaking, and sailing are popular among locals and tourists.

8. Maryborough: Hervey Bay is located near the historic town of Maryborough, which is known for its beautifully preserved colonial architecture. Visitors can explore its charming streets, visit heritage buildings, and learn about the region's rich history.

9. Climate: Hervey Bay enjoys a mild subtropical climate with warm summers and mild winters. The average summer temperature ranges from 22 to 29 degrees Celsius (72 to 84 degrees Fahrenheit), while winter temperatures range from 10 to 22 degrees Celsius (50 to 72 degrees Fahrenheit).

10. Gateway to the Great Barrier Reef: Hervey Bay serves as a gateway to the southern region of the Great Barrier Reef. Visitors can take day trips or multi-day tours to explore this world-renowned natural wonder, which is home to diverse marine life and vibrant coral reefs.

Overall, Hervey Bay offers a unique blend of natural beauty, outdoor activities, and relaxed coastal lifestyle, making it a popular destination for tourists seeking a quintessential Australian beach experience.

FRASER ISLAND

Fraser Island, located off the eastern coast of Queensland, Australia, is the largest sand island in the world and a UNESCO World Heritage site. Here is some detailed and concise information about Fraser Island:

1. Location and Size: Fraser Island is situated approximately 200 kilometres (124 miles) north of

Brisbane. It stretches over an area of about 1,840 square kilometres (710 square miles) and spans about 123 kilometres (76 miles) in length.

2. Unique Natural Features: Fraser Island is renowned for its exceptional natural features. It boasts stunning white sandy beaches, crystal-clear freshwater lakes, ancient rainforests, and towering sand dunes. The island's diverse ecosystems support a wide array of flora and fauna, including several species of wildlife.

3. Maheno Shipwreck: One of the most iconic landmarks on Fraser Island is the Maheno Shipwreck. The rusting remains of the SS Maheno, a luxury liner that washed ashore in 1935, can be found on the island's eastern beach. It has become a popular spot for photography and exploration.

4. 75 Mile Beach: Fraser Island's eastern beach, known as 75 Mile Beach, is a designated highway and an adventure lover's paradise. It serves as the main thoroughfare for vehicles exploring the island's attractions, including the Pinnacles

coloured sand cliffs, the Champagne Pools, and the Eli Creek.

5. Freshwater Lakes: Fraser Island is home to several stunning freshwater lakes, including Lake McKenzie, Lake Wabby, and Lake Birrabeen. These crystal-clear lakes are surrounded by pristine white sands and provide an ideal setting for swimming, picnicking, and relaxing.

6. Rainforests: The island features lush rainforests that grow in the sandy soil, a unique phenomenon. The Central Station Rainforest and Wanggoolba Creek offer visitors a chance to explore these ancient forests, which are home to rare plants and wildlife.

7. Wildlife: Fraser Island is a haven for wildlife enthusiasts. The island is home to a diverse range of animal species, including dingoes, wallabies, echidnas, and over 350 bird species. Visitors can spot these animals in their natural habitat while exploring the island.

8. Aboriginal Heritage: Fraser Island has significant cultural and historical importance to the Butchulla people, the traditional owners of the land. The island is rich in Aboriginal heritage, with numerous cultural sites and artefacts.

9. Adventure Activities: Fraser Island offers a plethora of adventure activities for thrill-seekers. Visitors can go four-wheel driving along the sandy tracks, embark on guided bushwalks, take scenic flights over the island, or try their hand at fishing in the island's freshwater streams.

10. Camping and Accommodation: Fraser Island provides camping facilities at various locations, including beachside campsites and designated camping areas. There are also resorts and lodges available for those seeking more comfortable accommodation options.

Fraser Island's unique natural beauty, diverse ecosystems, and rich cultural heritage make it a popular destination for nature lovers, adventure enthusiasts, and those seeking a truly unforgettable experience in Queensland, Australia.

LADY ELLIOT ISLAND

Lady Elliot Island is a small coral cay located at the southern end of the Great Barrier Reef in Queensland, Australia. Here is some detailed and concise information about Lady Elliot Island:

1. Location: Lady Elliot Island is situated approximately 80 kilometres (50 miles) northeast of Bundaberg in the southern region of the Great Barrier Reef. It is known as the "Home of the Manta Ray" due to the abundance of these majestic creatures in the surrounding waters.

2. Size and Accessibility: The island covers an area of about 45 hectares (110 acres) and is relatively small in size. It is accessible via scenic flights from Bundaberg, Hervey Bay, or the Gold Coast, as well as by private aircraft or boat charters.

3. Marine Life and Snorkelling: Lady Elliot Island is renowned for its pristine and diverse marine ecosystem. It offers excellent snorkelling opportunities, allowing visitors to explore vibrant coral reefs teeming with tropical fish, turtles, and

other marine creatures. The island's resident manta rays are a major highlight.

4. Manta Ray Research and Conservation: Lady Elliot Island is a hub for manta ray research and conservation. The island's Manta Ray Research and Conservation Project provides valuable insights into the behaviour, migration patterns, and conservation of these magnificent creatures. Visitors can learn about manta rays and participate in research activities.

5. Birdlife: Lady Elliot Island is a sanctuary for birdlife, with over 57 species of birds recorded on the island. It is particularly important as a breeding site for seabirds, including nesting colonies of wedge-tailed shearwaters and black noddies.

6. Eco-Friendly Resort: The island is home to an eco-friendly resort that offers accommodation options ranging from eco-cabins to glamping tents. The resort follows sustainable practices and operates in harmony with the island's fragile ecosystem.

7. Turtle Encounters: Lady Elliot Island is a significant nesting site for green and loggerhead turtles. From November to March, visitors have the opportunity to witness turtles coming ashore to lay their eggs, and from January to March, hatchlings make their way to the ocean.

8. Guided Tours and Activities: The island offers guided tours and activities, including reef walks, snorkelling tours, glass-bottom boat tours, and educational presentations about the marine environment. Visitors can also participate in night-time turtle encounters.

9. Conservation Efforts: Lady Elliot Island is dedicated to conservation and sustainability. The island's management implements measures to minimise the ecological impact of visitors and works towards preserving the natural environment and marine life.

10. Day Trips and Overnight Stays: Visitors can choose to visit Lady Elliot Island for a day trip from the mainland or opt for overnight stays to fully

experience the island's tranquillity and natural wonders.

Lady Elliot Island provides a unique and immersive experience for nature enthusiasts, snorkelers, and those seeking an intimate encounter with the Great Barrier Reef's diverse marine life. With its focus on conservation and research, the island offers a glimpse into the delicate balance of the reef ecosystem and the importance of protecting it for future generations.

BUNDABERG AND MON REPOS TURTLE CENTRE

Bundaberg is a city located on the east coast of Queensland, Australia. It is known for its sugar cane industry, rum distilleries, and as a gateway to the Southern Great Barrier Reef. Here is some detailed and concise information about Bundaberg and the Mon Repos Turtle Centre:

1. Location: Bundaberg is situated approximately 360 kilometres (225 miles) north of Brisbane, making it easily accessible for visitors travelling along the Queensland coast.

2. Sugar Cane and Rum: Bundaberg is renowned for its sugar cane industry, with vast plantations surrounding the city. The region is also famous for Bundaberg Rum, a popular Australian rum brand that has been produced in the area since 1888. Visitors can tour the Bundaberg Rum Distillery and learn about the rum-making process.

3. Southern Great Barrier Reef: Bundaberg serves as a gateway to the Southern Great Barrier Reef. From the city, visitors can embark on boat tours to explore the stunning coral reefs, swim with marine life, and snorkel or dive in the crystal-clear waters of Lady Musgrave Island and Lady Elliot Island.

4. Mon Repos Turtle Centre: Mon Repos Turtle Centre, located near Bundaberg, is an important conservation site for marine turtles, particularly the endangered loggerhead turtles. It is the largest turtle rookery on the east coast of Australia and

offers visitors a unique opportunity to witness turtle nesting and hatching.

5. Turtle Nesting and Hatching: From November to March, female turtles come ashore at Mon Repos Beach to lay their eggs in the sand. Visitors can join guided tours at night to witness these nesting rituals. From January to March, the hatchlings emerge from their nests and make their way to the ocean, providing a magical spectacle.

6. Interpretive Centre: The Mon Repos Turtle Centre features an interpretive centre where visitors can learn about the life cycle and behaviour of turtles through informative displays and exhibits. The centre also conducts educational programs and activities for all ages.

7. Turtle Encounter Experiences: The Mon Repos Turtle Centre offers a variety of turtle encounter experiences, including guided tours to witness nesting or hatching, as well as early-morning hatchling releases. These experiences provide an intimate and educational encounter with these fascinating creatures.

8. Environmental Conservation: The Mon Repos Turtle Centre plays a crucial role in turtle conservation efforts. The centre monitors and protects the nesting turtles and their eggs, educates the public about turtle conservation, and conducts research to better understand and preserve these endangered species.

9. Beach and Coastal Environment: The Mon Repos Beach, where the turtle encounters take place, is a pristine stretch of sandy coastline. Visitors can enjoy the beach during the day, taking in the natural beauty and tranquillity of the area.

10. Visitor Facilities: The Mon Repos Turtle Centre provides visitor facilities, including a gift shop, picnic areas, and amenities. There are also knowledgeable staff and volunteers available to provide information and answer questions about the turtles and the surrounding environment.

Bundaberg and the Mon Repos Turtle Centre offer a unique combination of cultural heritage, natural beauty, and wildlife conservation. Visitors have the opportunity to explore the city's rich history, sample the local rum, and witness the extraordinary journey of nesting and hatching turtles at Mon Repos.

MARYBOROUGH HERITAGE CITY

Maryborough is a charming heritage city located on the Fraser Coast in Queensland, Australia. It is known for its rich history, beautifully preserved colonial architecture, and strong connection to the author of Mary Poppins, P.L. Travers. Here is some detailed and concise information about Maryborough Heritage City:

1. Location: Maryborough is situated approximately 255 kilometres (158 miles) north of Brisbane. It is nestled on the banks of the Mary River, about 20 kilometres (12 miles) inland from the coast.

2. Colonial Architecture: Maryborough boasts a wealth of stunning colonial architecture, with many buildings dating back to the 1800s. The city's streets are lined with well-preserved heritage buildings, including ornate Victorian-era facades, charming timber cottages, and grand public structures.

3. Wharf Precinct: The Wharf Precinct in Maryborough is a hub of historical significance and cultural activity. It features the iconic Maryborough Wharf, which was once a bustling port for steamships. Visitors can explore the wharf area, learn about the city's maritime history, and enjoy riverside dining and entertainment.

4. Mary Poppins Connection: Maryborough is the birthplace of P.L. Travers, the author of the famous Mary Poppins series. The city pays tribute to this literary connection through various attractions, including the Mary Poppins statue and the Story Bank, which offers an immersive experience into the world of Mary Poppins.

5. Customs House and Bond Store Museum: The Customs House, a grand heritage building overlooking the river, now houses the Bond Store Museum. This museum showcases the history of Maryborough as a port and delves into the stories of immigration, trade, and the region's cultural heritage.

6. Queens Park and Mary River Parklands: Queens Park is a beautiful parkland in the heart of Maryborough. It features well-manicured gardens, picnic areas, playgrounds, and walking paths. Nearby, the Mary River Parklands offer riverside parklands and scenic viewpoints, perfect for relaxing and enjoying the natural surroundings.

7. Maryborough Military and Colonial Museum: The Maryborough Military and Colonial Museum is a must-visit for history enthusiasts. It houses an extensive collection of military artefacts, including weapons, uniforms, and vehicles, as well as exhibits on the city's colonial past.

8. Portside Heritage Gateway: The Portside Heritage Gateway is an informative and interactive

centre that provides visitors with a glimpse into Maryborough's history, indigenous heritage, and the region's importance as a port and trading hub.

9. Festivals and Events: Maryborough hosts a range of vibrant festivals and events throughout the year. The Mary Poppins Festival, Relish Food and Wine Festival, and Maryborough Open House are just a few examples of the city's lively calendar of cultural celebrations.

10. Heritage Walks and Tours: Visitors can explore Maryborough's heritage at their own pace by following the Heritage Walks, which guide them through the city's historic streets and showcase its architectural gems. Guided tours are also available to delve deeper into the city's history and stories.

Maryborough Heritage City offers a captivating blend of colonial charm, cultural significance, and historical attractions. Its well-preserved architecture, Mary Poppins connection, and immersive museums make it a delightful destination for those seeking to step back in time and appreciate Queensland's rich heritage.

OUTBACK QUEENSLAND

LONGREACH AND QANTAS FOUNDERS MUSEUM

Longreach is a town located in central Queensland, Australia. It is known for its rich history and connection to the Australian aviation industry. One of the key attractions in Longreach is the Qantas Founders Museum, which showcases the history of Qantas, Australia's national airline.

Qantas Founders Museum is dedicated to preserving and showcasing the heritage of Qantas Airways, one of the world's oldest and most respected airlines. The museum is located at the site where Qantas was founded in 1920 as the Queensland and Northern Territory Aerial Services Limited.

The museum offers visitors a range of exhibits and experiences that highlight the growth and development of Qantas over the years. It features an impressive collection of aircraft, including a fully restored Boeing 747, a Boeing 707, a DC-3, and a Catalina flying boat. These aircraft give visitors a chance to see the evolution of aviation technology up close.

One of the museum's main attractions is the "Airpark" exhibition, which displays several historic aircraft in an outdoor setting. Visitors can explore the interiors of some of these aircraft and learn about their significance in aviation history. The museum also houses various galleries that showcase Qantas memorabilia, photographs, and interactive displays that educate visitors about the airline's pioneering spirit and achievements.

Additionally, the Qantas Founders Museum offers guided tours that take visitors behind the scenes of the national airline. These tours provide insight into the inner workings of Qantas, including visits to the Boeing 747 and the airline's maintenance facilities.

Overall, the Qantas Founders Museum in Longreach is a must-visit destination for aviation enthusiasts and anyone interested in learning about the remarkable story of Qantas Airways. It offers a unique opportunity to explore the history of Australian aviation and appreciate the accomplishments of this iconic airline.

MOUNT ISA AND OUTBACK MINING

Mount Isa is a city located in the Gulf Country region of Queensland, Australia. It is renowned for its rich mineral deposits and is often referred to as the "Outback mining capital" of the country. Here is some detailed yet concise information on Mount Isa and outback mining:

Mount Isa:
- Mount Isa is the largest city in western Queensland and is situated on the Leichhardt River.
- It was established in 1923 following the discovery of significant mineral deposits, primarily copper, lead, zinc, and silver.

- The mining industry has played a crucial role in the development and economy of the city, attracting a diverse population of miners and supporting infrastructure.
- Mount Isa is also known for its stunning landscapes, including the rugged Selwyn Ranges and the picturesque Lake Moondarra.
- The city offers a range of outdoor activities, such as fishing, camping, and exploring the nearby national parks.

Outback Mining:
- Outback mining refers to the mining activities conducted in remote and arid regions of Australia, such as Mount Isa and other areas in Queensland's outback.
- These regions are characterised by vast expanses of uninhabited land and are rich in various minerals, including copper, gold, silver, lead, zinc, and uranium.
- Mining operations in the outback often require significant infrastructure and logistical challenges due to the remote location and harsh environmental conditions.

- The mining industry in the outback has contributed significantly to the economic growth of regional areas, providing employment opportunities and supporting local communities.
- It is a vital sector for Queensland's economy and has helped establish the state as a significant player in the global mining industry.

In summary, Mount Isa is a city in Queensland known for its mining industry and abundant mineral deposits. The region's outback mining activities have been instrumental in the city's growth and development, attracting miners and supporting infrastructure. The outback mining industry plays a crucial role in Queensland's economy and contributes to the state's reputation as a major global mining hub.

WINTON AND AUSTRALIAN AGE OF DINOSAURS MUSEUM

Winton is a small town located in central western Queensland, Australia. It is known for its rich paleontological history and as the birthplace of Waltzing Matilda, Australia's unofficial national anthem. Here is some detailed yet concise information on Winton and the Australian Age of Dinosaurs Museum:

Winton:
- Winton is situated in the heart of Queensland's outback and is surrounded by vast landscapes, including red earth plains, rocky escarpments, and ancient gorges.
- The town has a strong connection to Australia's pioneering and bush heritage, and it holds a significant place in the history of the country's cattle industry.
- Winton gained worldwide recognition as the birthplace of the iconic Australian folk song, Waltzing Matilda, composed by Banjo Paterson in 1895.
- The town offers a range of attractions and activities, including heritage sites, museums, art galleries, and opportunities to experience outback life and culture.

Australian Age of Dinosaurs Museum:

- The Australian Age of Dinosaurs Museum (AAOD) is located near Winton and is one of the most significant dinosaur museums in Australia.
- The museum focuses on the fossils and dinosaur discoveries made in the Winton region, which is renowned for its wealth of dinosaur fossils.
- The AAOD museum complex consists of several buildings, including the Collection Room, the Laboratory, and the Dinosaur Canyon, which features life-size dinosaur replicas.
- Visitors to the museum can participate in guided tours, fossil preparation sessions, and even "Dinosaur Dig" experiences, where they can join palaeontologists on real fossil digs.
- The museum's collection includes dinosaur skeletons, fossils, and exhibits that provide insights into the prehistoric world and the evolution of dinosaurs in Australia.
- The AAOD museum aims to educate the public about the ancient history of the region and the ongoing scientific research being conducted to uncover more about Australia's dinosaurs.

In summary, Winton is a historic outback town in Queensland, known for its pioneering heritage and as the birthplace of Waltzing Matilda. The Australian Age of Dinosaurs Museum, located near Winton, is a premier dinosaur museum that showcases the region's rich paleontological history and offers visitors the opportunity to learn about and engage with Australia's prehistoric past.

BIRDSVILLE AND THE BIRDSVILLE TRACK

Birdsville is a remote town located in the southwestern corner of Queensland, Australia. It is known for its isolation, rugged landscapes, and iconic outback events. Here is some detailed yet concise information on Birdsville and the Birdsville Track:

Birdsville:
- Birdsville is situated on the edge of the Simpson Desert, surrounded by vast stretches of red sand dunes and desert plains.

- The town is known for its extreme temperatures, ranging from scorching hot summers to chilly winters, characteristic of the Australian outback.
- Birdsville is famous for hosting the Birdsville Races, an annual horse racing event that attracts visitors from all over Australia and beyond.
- The town is also a popular stopover for travellers exploring the outback, providing essential services and amenities such as fuel, accommodation, and food.
- Birdsville's population is small, but it swells significantly during peak tourist seasons and major events.

Birdsville Track:
- The Birdsville Track is an iconic outback road that stretches approximately 517 kilometres (321 miles) from Birdsville to Marree in South Australia.
- It is one of Australia's most famous outback tracks, known for its remoteness and challenging conditions.
- The track traverses arid landscapes, red sand dunes, gibber plains, and occasional floodplains, offering stunning outback scenery along the way.

- It is a historic stock route used for moving cattle between Birdsville and Marree, dating back to the late 19th century.

- Travelling the Birdsville Track is a popular adventure for 4WD enthusiasts and tourists seeking an authentic outback experience.

- It is recommended to have a well-equipped vehicle, sufficient supplies, and knowledge of outback travel before embarking on the journey.

In summary, Birdsville is a remote outback town in Queensland, known for its isolation, extreme temperatures, and the famous Birdsville Races. The Birdsville Track, a historic outback road, connects Birdsville to Marree in South Australia, providing travellers with a challenging yet rewarding adventure through stunning outback landscapes.

UNDARA LAVA TUBES AND NATIONAL PARK

The Undara Lava Tubes and National Park are located in far north Queensland, Australia. They are renowned for their geological significance and unique underground formations. Here is some detailed yet concise information on the Undara Lava Tubes and National Park:

Undara Lava Tubes:
- The Undara Lava Tubes are a natural phenomenon formed by volcanic activity that occurred around 190,000 years ago.
- The tubes were created when lava flowed from the Undara Volcano and formed tunnels and caves as the outer layers cooled and hardened while the molten lava continued to flow underneath.
- The Undara Lava Tubes are one of the longest and best-preserved lava tube systems in the world, spanning over 160 kilometres (100 miles) in total length.
- The tubes boast impressive geological features, including magnificent arches, tunnels, and

caverns that showcase the raw power of ancient volcanic eruptions.

- The tubes are home to a unique ecosystem, supporting a variety of plant and animal life, including microbats, insects, and ferns.

Undara Volcanic National Park:
- The Undara Volcanic National Park encompasses the Undara Lava Tubes and the surrounding volcanic landscapes.
- The national park offers visitors a chance to explore and appreciate the geological wonders of the lava tubes through guided tours and walks.
- Guided tours take visitors deep into the underground network, allowing them to witness the impressive scale and intricate formations of the lava tubes.
- The national park also features a range of walking trails, showcasing the diverse flora and fauna of the region, including eucalypt forests and savannah woodlands.
- Visitors can enjoy camping facilities within the park, immersing themselves in the unique outback environment and experiencing the tranquillity of the Australian bush.

In summary, the Undara Lava Tubes and National Park in Queensland are a testament to the region's volcanic history and geological marvels. The lava tubes provide an awe-inspiring underground experience, while the national park offers opportunities to explore the surrounding volcanic landscapes and appreciate the diverse flora and fauna of the area. It is a remarkable destination for nature lovers and those fascinated by the Earth's geological wonders.

INDIGENOUS CULTURE AND HISTORY

ABORIGINAL CULTURAL EXPERIENCES

Aboriginal Cultural Experiences in Queensland offer a unique opportunity to engage with the rich cultural heritage and traditions of Australia's Aboriginal peoples. Here is a brief overview of these experiences:

1. Traditional Welcome/Ceremonies: Many Aboriginal cultural experiences begin with a traditional Welcome to Country or Smoking Ceremony. These ceremonies acknowledge and pay respect to the traditional custodians of the land and cleanse the area spiritually.

2. Cultural Centers and Tours: Aboriginal cultural centres and museums in Queensland provide insights into Aboriginal history, art, and

traditions. Visitors can participate in guided tours, watch cultural performances, view artefacts, and learn about Dreamtime stories.

3. Art and Craft Workshops: Aboriginal art is renowned for its vibrant colours and intricate designs. Cultural experiences often include workshops where participants can learn traditional art techniques such as dot painting, weaving, or carving. These workshops allow for hands-on experiences and a deeper understanding of Aboriginal art forms.

4. Bush Tucker Experiences: Aboriginal people have a rich knowledge of native plants and their uses. Bush tucker experiences provide an opportunity to learn about traditional food gathering, cooking techniques, and taste unique flavours of native ingredients. These experiences may include guided bush walks, hunting demonstrations, or cooking demonstrations.

5. Guided Cultural Walks: Aboriginal guides offer guided walks through significant cultural sites, such as rock art sites or ancestral lands. They

provide insights into the spiritual and historical significance of these places, sharing Dreamtime stories and explaining the connection between the land and Aboriginal culture.

6. Performance and Dance: Aboriginal cultural experiences often feature traditional performances and dance shows. These showcases highlight traditional dances, songs, and storytelling methods passed down through generations. Visitors can witness the beauty and significance of Aboriginal performing arts.

7. Cultural Immersion Programs: For a more in-depth experience, some cultural centres and communities offer immersive programs where visitors can stay overnight and participate in everyday activities alongside Aboriginal community members. These programs provide a unique opportunity to learn about traditional practices, language, and gain a deeper understanding of Aboriginal life.

It's important to note that each Aboriginal cultural experience is unique, reflecting the diverse cultures and traditions of different Aboriginal groups across Queensland. It is recommended to research and engage with reputable cultural organisations or tour operators to ensure an authentic and respectful experience.

TJAPUKAI ABORIGINAL CULTURAL PARK

Tjapukai Aboriginal Cultural Park in Queensland is a renowned cultural attraction that offers immersive experiences to learn about the culture and traditions of the local Aboriginal people. Here is some detailed and concise information about the park:

1. Location: Tjapukai Aboriginal Cultural Park is situated in Caravonica, just 15 minutes' drive from Cairns in Queensland, Australia. Its location in the picturesque rainforest provides a stunning backdrop for cultural exploration.

2. Cultural Experiences: The park offers a range of interactive experiences that allow visitors to engage with Aboriginal culture. These include traditional dances, didgeridoo performances, and storytelling sessions. Visitors can witness vibrant performances that showcase the art of dance, music, and storytelling that have been passed down through generations.

3. Art and Craft Workshops: At Tjapukai, visitors can participate in hands-on workshops to learn traditional art and craft techniques. These workshops provide an opportunity to create unique Aboriginal artworks, such as dot paintings or boomerangs, under the guidance of experienced Aboriginal artists.

4. Cultural Demonstrations: The park offers various demonstrations that provide insights into Aboriginal traditions and practices. Visitors can learn about traditional hunting and gathering methods, the use of native plants for medicinal purposes, and the preparation of bush tucker (traditional food).

5. Cultural Village: Tjapukai features a cultural village where visitors can explore different aspects of Aboriginal culture. They can visit traditional dwellings, witness ceremonial performances, and interact with Aboriginal guides who share their knowledge and answer questions.

6. Night Fire Experience: The Night Fire Experience is a popular event at Tjapukai, offering an evening of entertainment and cultural immersion. Visitors can enjoy a buffet dinner while watching performances that include fire-making demonstrations, dances, and live music.

7. Dreamtime Walk: The Dreamtime Walk is a guided tour that takes visitors through the park, providing insights into the ancient traditions, Dreamtime stories, and spiritual beliefs of the local Aboriginal people. The tour covers various aspects of Aboriginal culture, including art, music, and language.

8. Cultural Heritage Museum: Tjapukai's Cultural Heritage Museum displays a collection of artefacts, photographs, and artworks that highlight the rich

history and cultural significance of the local Aboriginal communities. It offers a deeper understanding of their traditions, history, and ongoing contributions.

Tjapukai Aboriginal Cultural Park aims to foster a greater understanding and appreciation of Aboriginal culture. It provides an engaging and educational experience that allows visitors to connect with the heritage and traditions of the local Aboriginal people in a respectful and immersive manner.

QUINKAN CULTURAL CENTRE AND LAURA ROCK ART

The Quinkan Cultural Centre and Laura Rock Art in Queensland are significant cultural sites that offer a glimpse into the ancient Aboriginal heritage and rock art of the region. Here is some detailed and concise information about these attractions:

1. Quinkan Cultural Centre: The Quinkan Cultural Centre is located in Laura, a small town in Queensland's Cape York Peninsula. The centre serves as an educational facility and a gateway to the nearby Quinkan rock art sites.

2. Exhibitions and Interpretive Displays: The cultural centre features informative exhibitions and interpretive displays that provide an in-depth understanding of the local Aboriginal culture, including the rock art traditions of the Quinkan people. Visitors can learn about the history, spirituality, and significance of the rock art through visual displays, artefacts, and multimedia presentations.

3. Quinkan Rock Art: The Quinkan rock art sites are a UNESCO World Heritage-listed cultural landscape. These sites are known for their stunning and well-preserved rock art, which showcases the artistic skills and cultural expression of the Aboriginal people who inhabited the area for thousands of years.

4. Guided Tours: The Quinkan Cultural Centre offers guided tours to the rock art sites. Knowledgeable guides provide insights into the different styles of rock art, their meanings, and the cultural context in which they were created. Visitors can explore multiple sites, including Split Rock and Giant Horse, and witness the diverse range of rock art imagery.

5. Rock Art Styles: The rock art at Laura displays various styles, including the Quinkan figures, dynamic human figures with elongated bodies and large eyes. Other styles include the elegant Dynamic figures and the mysterious contact figures, depicting human-animal hybrids. These styles offer unique glimpses into the spiritual beliefs and cultural practices of the Aboriginal people.

6. Cultural Significance: The Quinkan rock art is of immense cultural significance to the Traditional Owners, the Aboriginal people of the Laura region. It serves as a connection to their ancestral past, conveying stories, ceremonies, and the Dreamtime

mythology that has shaped their identity and worldview.

7. Preservation and Conservation: The Quinkan Cultural Centre and local Indigenous communities actively collaborate to preserve and protect the rock art sites. Conservation efforts include the use of technology to monitor the art's condition and community-led initiatives to ensure its long-term preservation.

Visiting the Quinkan Cultural Centre and exploring the nearby rock art sites provides a unique opportunity to appreciate and learn about the ancient Aboriginal cultural heritage of the region. It is important to respect the sites and follow any guidelines or restrictions in place to ensure the preservation of these significant cultural treasures.

CULTURAL TOURS AND GUIDED EXPERIENCES

Cultural tours and guided experiences in Queensland offer visitors a chance to explore and engage with the diverse cultural heritage of the region. Here is some detailed and concise information about these tours and experiences:

1. Indigenous Cultural Tours: Indigenous cultural tours provide insights into the traditions, art, and spirituality of Aboriginal and Torres Strait Islander peoples. Led by knowledgeable Indigenous guides, these tours often include visits to significant cultural sites, bush tucker experiences, storytelling, and traditional performances.

2. Heritage Walking Tours: Heritage walking tours are available in many cities and towns across Queensland, allowing visitors to explore the historical and cultural landmarks. These tours often focus on colonial history, architecture, and local stories, providing a deeper understanding of the region's heritage.

3. Food and Wine Tours: Queensland's diverse culinary scene is often showcased through food and wine tours. These guided experiences take visitors on a gastronomic journey, introducing them to local produce, traditional cuisines, and unique flavours. They may include visits to farmers' markets, wineries, breweries, and food tastings.

4. Art and Cultural Workshops: Queensland is home to a thriving arts community, and art and cultural workshops offer hands-on experiences in various art forms. Visitors can learn techniques such as painting, ceramics, weaving, or printmaking from local artists and gain insight into the cultural significance of these art forms.

5. Eco and Indigenous Tourism Experiences: Queensland's natural beauty and rich Indigenous heritage often intersect in eco and Indigenous tourism experiences. These guided tours focus on sustainable practices and provide opportunities to explore pristine environments, such as rainforests,

coastal areas, and the Great Barrier Reef, while learning about Indigenous connections to the land.

6. Historical Site Tours: Queensland has numerous historical sites that reflect its colonial past and early settlement. Guided tours of heritage sites, including old buildings, museums, and archaeological sites, offer a glimpse into the history, architecture, and social context of the region.

7. Multicultural Festivals and Events: Queensland hosts a wide range of multicultural festivals and events throughout the year, celebrating the state's cultural diversity. Visitors can immerse themselves in vibrant celebrations featuring music, dance, food, and customs from various cultural backgrounds.

These tours and guided experiences provide opportunities to engage with the diverse cultures and traditions present in Queensland. They allow visitors to gain a deeper appreciation for the region's rich cultural heritage while fostering cross-cultural understanding and connection.

FOOD AND WINE

EXPERIENCES

SEAFOOD DELIGHTS AND
COASTAL CUISINE

Queensland, located in northeastern Australia, is renowned for its spectacular coastline and abundant marine resources, making it a seafood lover's paradise. The region offers a diverse range of seafood delights and coastal cuisine that showcase the freshness and flavours of the ocean. Here's a brief overview of the culinary experiences you can expect in Queensland:

1. Barramundi: Barramundi is an iconic fish in Queensland and is known for its delicate flavour and firm, moist flesh. It can be prepared in various ways, including grilling, pan-frying, or oven-baking, and is often served with citrus-infused sauces or tropical fruit salsas.

2. Mud Crabs: Queensland's estuaries and mangrove-lined creeks are home to delicious mud crabs. These large crustaceans are prized for their sweet and succulent meat. Mud crabs are typically steamed or boiled and served with a side of tangy chilli or garlic butter sauce.

3. Moreton Bay Bugs: Moreton Bay bugs, also known as bay lobsters or slipper lobsters, are a local delicacy found in the waters off Queensland's coast. They have a delicate flavour similar to lobster and are often grilled with a herb and garlic butter marinade or used in pasta dishes and seafood salads.

4. Prawns: Queensland is famous for its succulent and flavoursome prawns. Whether served chilled with a zesty cocktail sauce or tossed in a spicy stir-fry, prawns are a popular choice among seafood enthusiasts.

5. Oysters: The pristine waters of Queensland's coastline yield some of the finest oysters in Australia. Varieties like Pacific oysters and Sydney rock oysters are commonly found, and they can be

enjoyed fresh on the half-shell or incorporated into various seafood dishes.

6. Coral Trout: Coral trout is a highly sought-after reef fish known for its delicate, flaky white flesh. It is often grilled, pan-fried, or baked whole and served with a squeeze of lemon or accompanied by tropical fruit salsas.

7. Balmain Bugs: Balmain bugs, also called shovel-nose lobsters, are another delicious crustacean found in Queensland's waters. They have a sweet, firm meat that is often grilled, barbecued, or used in seafood pasta dishes.

8. Indigenous Cuisine: Queensland also offers the opportunity to explore indigenous coastal cuisine. Aboriginal and Torres Strait Islander cultures incorporate a wide array of seafood in their traditional dishes, such as barramundi, mussels, and shellfish. Indigenous dining experiences often showcase unique cooking techniques and flavours derived from native herbs and spices.

In addition to these specific seafood delicacies, Queensland's coastal cuisine features a diverse range of dishes influenced by international flavours. From freshly shucked oysters to barbecued seafood platters, visitors to Queensland can indulge in an array of seafood delights that highlight the region's natural bounty and culinary creativity.

TROPICAL FRUITS AND LOCAL PRODUCE

Queensland, known as the Sunshine State of Australia, is blessed with a tropical climate that allows for the cultivation of a wide variety of delicious fruits and fresh local produce. Here is a brief overview of the tropical fruits and local produce you can find in Queensland:

1. Mangoes: Queensland is renowned for its juicy and aromatic mangoes. The region's warm climate and fertile soil provide ideal conditions for mango cultivation. During the summer months

(November to March), you can enjoy a wide range of mango varieties, including Kensington Pride, R2E2, and Calypso. They are perfect for enjoying fresh, in smoothies, or as a topping for desserts.

2. Pineapples: Another tropical delight in Queensland is the pineapple. The state produces a significant portion of Australia's pineapples, known for their sweet, tangy flavour. Queensland's pineapples are often enjoyed fresh, juiced, or incorporated into tropical fruit salads and desserts.

3. Pawpaw (Papaya): Pawpaw is a tropical fruit that thrives in Queensland's warm climate. It has a vibrant orange flesh and a sweet, slightly musty flavour. Pawpaw is commonly eaten fresh, included in fruit salads, or blended into refreshing smoothies.

4. Bananas: Queensland is one of Australia's leading banana-growing regions. The state's subtropical and tropical zones provide the perfect conditions for banana plantations. Queensland bananas are known for their creamy texture and

sweet flavour. They can be eaten as a snack, added to breakfast bowls, or used in baking.

5. Avocados: Avocado orchards are scattered throughout Queensland, with the fruit thriving in the state's warm and sunny climate. Queensland avocados are creamy, rich, and full of flavour. They are used in a variety of dishes, from classic avocado toast to guacamole and salads.

6. Macadamia Nuts: Queensland is home to the native macadamia tree, and the state produces a significant portion of Australia's macadamia nuts. These buttery and crunchy nuts are widely used in both sweet and savoury dishes, including desserts, salads, and roasted snacks.

7. Passionfruit: Passionfruit is a popular tropical fruit in Queensland, known for its tangy and aromatic flavour. The state's warm climate allows for the abundant production of passionfruit. They are often enjoyed fresh, used in desserts, added to tropical cocktails, or turned into tangy sauces and dressings.

8. Local Produce: Queensland's fertile lands also yield a diverse range of fresh local produce. From vibrant vegetables like tomatoes, capsicums (bell peppers), and sweet potatoes to herbs, such as basil and lemongrass, you'll find an abundance of locally grown ingredients to enhance your culinary creations.

Visitors to Queensland can explore local farmers' markets, roadside stalls, and tropical fruit farms to experience the flavours of these delightful tropical fruits and local produce. Whether you're enjoying a refreshing mango on a warm summer day or indulging in a delicious avocado dish, Queensland's tropical fruits and local produce offer a vibrant and delicious culinary experience.

WINE TASTING IN QUEENSLAND WINERIES

Queensland may not be as well-known as other Australian regions like South Australia or Victoria when it comes to wine production, but it still boasts several wineries that offer unique and enjoyable wine tasting experiences. Here's a brief overview of wine tasting in Queensland wineries:

1. Granite Belt Region: Located in the southeastern part of the state, the Granite Belt region is Queensland's premier wine-producing area. It is known for its cool climate, high altitude, and granite-rich soils, which are conducive to grape cultivation. The region specialises in producing a range of wines, including Shiraz, Cabernet Sauvignon, Chardonnay, and alternative varietals like Verdelho and Petit Verdot. Visitors can explore the numerous cellar doors and wineries in the area and enjoy wine tastings accompanied by picturesque vineyard views.

2. South Burnett Region: Situated north of the Sunshine Coast, the South Burnett region is gaining recognition for its wine production. The area benefits from a warm climate and fertile soils, which are suitable for growing a variety of grapes. The region is known for producing wines such as Shiraz, Merlot, Chardonnay, and Verdelho. Wine enthusiasts can visit cellar doors and wineries in

the South Burnett region to sample these wines and learn about the winemaking process.

3. Scenic Rim Region: The Scenic Rim, located near Brisbane, is a picturesque region that encompasses both rural and mountainous landscapes. While it is primarily known for its natural beauty, the area is also home to some wineries. These wineries produce a range of wines, including Chardonnay, Shiraz, and Verdelho. Wine tastings in the Scenic Rim offer a chance to savour wines while enjoying the region's stunning vistas and relaxed atmosphere.

4. Tropical North Queensland: In the far north of Queensland, near Cairns and the Great Barrier Reef, you can find wineries that take advantage of the unique tropical climate. These wineries produce wines that showcase the region's distinctive characteristics. Tropical fruit wines, such as mango wine, passion fruit wine, and lychee wine, are popular choices in this area. Wine tasting in tropical north Queensland offers a different experience, allowing visitors to sample unconventional and fruit-forward wines.

During wine tastings in Queensland wineries, visitors can expect to learn about the winemaking process, the characteristics of the wines produced in the region, and the specific vineyard practices. Winery tours and guided tastings are often available, providing an opportunity to gain insight into the local wine industry and discover unique flavours.

It's worth noting that while Queensland may not have the same wine reputation as some other Australian regions, its wineries offer a charming and often more intimate wine tasting experience. With beautiful landscapes, friendly hospitality, and a focus on local and unique varieties, wine enthusiasts can discover hidden gems and enjoy a memorable wine tasting journey in Queensland.

FOOD FESTIVALS AND FARMERS' MARKETS

Queensland, Australia, is known for its vibrant food culture and a plethora of food festivals and farmers' markets that celebrate local produce, culinary talents, and gastronomic delights. Here's a brief overview of some of the notable food festivals and farmers' markets in Queensland:

1. Noosa Food and Wine Festival: Held in the picturesque coastal town of Noosa, the Noosa Food and Wine Festival is a renowned event that showcases the region's exceptional food and wine scene. The festival features cooking demonstrations by celebrity chefs, wine tastings, local produce showcases, and gourmet dining experiences.

2. Regional Flavours: Regional Flavours is an annual food and wine festival held in Brisbane, the capital city of Queensland. The event highlights the diverse and abundant produce from across the state, with cooking demonstrations, food stalls,

and live entertainment. Regional Flavours offers an opportunity to sample the flavours of Queensland while enjoying a vibrant atmosphere.

3. Eat Street Northshore: Eat Street Northshore is a bustling night market located in Brisbane. It features a wide array of international street food stalls, live music, and a vibrant atmosphere. Visitors can savour a variety of flavours from around the world while strolling through the market's vibrant laneways.

4. Burleigh Farmers' Market: Situated on the Gold Coast, the Burleigh Farmers' Market is a popular destination for fresh produce and local artisanal products. The market offers a wide range of fruits, vegetables, baked goods, gourmet treats, and more. It's a great place to interact with local farmers, sample their products, and support the region's agricultural community.

5. The Rocklea Markets: Located in Brisbane, the Rocklea Markets is one of the largest fresh produce markets in Queensland. Open every Saturday, the market offers an extensive range of fruits,

vegetables, meat, seafood, and specialty items. It's a favourite spot for both locals and chefs looking for high-quality, locally sourced produce.

6. The Davies Park Market: Held in West End, Brisbane, the Davies Park Market is a popular weekend market known for its fresh produce, gourmet food stalls, and vibrant community atmosphere. Visitors can find an assortment of organic fruits and vegetables, artisanal bread, cheese, spices, and more.

7. Eumundi Markets: Located on the Sunshine Coast, the Eumundi Markets are a must-visit for locals and tourists alike. The markets feature a diverse range of stalls selling fresh produce, handmade crafts, clothing, and, of course, delectable food and snacks. The markets have a lively and bustling atmosphere, with live music adding to the vibrant ambiance.

These are just a few examples of the many food festivals and farmers' markets you can explore in Queensland. Whether you're looking to sample local produce, discover artisanal products, or indulge in diverse culinary experiences, Queensland's food festivals and farmers' markets offer a delightful showcase of the region's vibrant food culture and community spirit.

ADVENTURE AND OUTDOOR ACTIVITIES

GREAT BARRIER REEF ADVENTURES

Great Barrier Reef Adventures in Queensland offer visitors a chance to explore and experience one of the most remarkable natural wonders on the planet. Here is some detailed and concise information about Great Barrier Reef Adventures:

Location: The Great Barrier Reef is located off the coast of Queensland, Australia. It stretches over 2,300 kilometres (1,400 miles) along the northeast coast of the state.

Activities: Great Barrier Reef Adventures offer a wide range of activities for visitors to enjoy. Some popular activities include:

1. Snorkelling: Snorkelling allows you to observe the vibrant marine life up close. With a mask and snorkel, you can explore the shallow areas of the reef and witness the stunning coral formations and colourful fish.

2. Scuba Diving: Certified divers have the opportunity to dive into the deeper parts of the reef, where they can discover intricate coral gardens, swim alongside sea turtles, and encounter other fascinating marine creatures.

3. Reef Tours: Various tour operators offer day trips and multi-day excursions to the Great Barrier Reef. These tours typically include transportation to and from the reef, guided snorkelling or diving sessions, and sometimes additional activities like glass-bottom boat rides or helicopter tours.

4. Sailing and Cruising: For a more leisurely experience, visitors can embark on a sailing or cruising adventure. These trips allow you to relax on board, enjoy the breathtaking views, and even stop at different locations along the reef for snorkelling or diving.

5. Helicopter or Seaplane Tours: Taking to the skies provides a unique perspective of the Great Barrier Reef. Helicopter or seaplane tours offer aerial views of the reef's vast expanse, showcasing its breathtaking beauty from above.

Important Conservation Efforts: The Great Barrier Reef faces significant environmental challenges, including coral bleaching caused by climate change. As part of Great Barrier Reef Adventures, many operators actively promote sustainable practices and educate visitors about reef conservation. They emphasise the importance of responsible tourism to protect and preserve this delicate ecosystem.

Cairns and the Whitsunday Islands: Cairns and the Whitsunday Islands are popular departure points for Great Barrier Reef Adventures. Cairns offers easy access to the reef with numerous tour options, while the Whitsunday Islands provide a picturesque setting for reef exploration, surrounded by crystal-clear waters and stunning white-sand beaches.

Unique Marine Life: The Great Barrier Reef is home to a diverse range of marine life, including over 1,500 species of fish, 400 types of coral, and numerous other marine creatures like sea turtles, dolphins, sharks, and rays. It is also a significant breeding ground for various species, making it an important ecological hotspot.

Overall, Great Barrier Reef Adventures in Queensland provide an unforgettable experience, allowing visitors to immerse themselves in the beauty and wonder of this extraordinary natural treasure while fostering awareness of the need for its preservation.

HIKING AND BUSHWALKING TRAILS

Queensland offers a wide array of hiking and bushwalking trails that showcase the state's stunning landscapes and natural beauty. Here is some detailed yet concise information about hiking and bushwalking trails in Queensland:

1. Lamington National Park: Located in the Gold Coast hinterland, Lamington National Park is renowned for its diverse rainforest scenery. The park features several trails, including the popular Border Track, which stretches for 21 kilometres (13 miles) along the Queensland-New South Wales border. The O'Reilly's Rainforest Retreat provides a starting point for various walks, such as the Tree Top Walk and the Box Forest Circuit.

2. Daintree National Park: Situated in Far North Queensland, Daintree National Park is a UNESCO World Heritage site and one of the oldest rainforests on Earth. The park offers several trails, including the popular Jindalba Boardwalk, where visitors can immerse themselves in the lush rainforest and spot unique flora and fauna.

3. Carnarvon Gorge: Located in Carnarvon National Park, this iconic gorge features towering sandstone cliffs, ancient Aboriginal rock art sites, and a pristine creek. The main walking track, the

Carnarvon Gorge Great Walk, spans approximately 87 kilometres (54 miles) and can be completed over multiple days, or visitors can explore shorter walks, such as the Moss Garden and the Amphitheatre.

4. Mount Barney National Park: Situated in the Scenic Rim region, Mount Barney National Park offers challenging hikes for experienced bushwalkers. The summit of Mount Barney provides panoramic views, while the Lower Portals track leads to beautiful rock pools and waterfalls.

5. Whitsunday Great Walk: This multi-day hike takes adventurers through the lush rainforest of the Conway National Park and showcases the stunning Whitsunday Islands. The trail covers approximately 30 kilometres (18.6 miles) and offers breathtaking views of the surrounding islands and coastline.

6. Mount Warning Summit Trail: Located in Wollumbin National Park, just across the border in New South Wales but easily accessible from Queensland, this trail leads to the summit of

Mount Warning, an ancient volcanic remnant. Hikers can witness spectacular sunrises from the summit while enjoying sweeping views of the surrounding hinterland and coastline.

These are just a few examples of the many hiking and bushwalking trails in Queensland. Each trail offers a unique experience, from rainforest adventures to mountain summits and coastal walks. It's essential to check the trail conditions, carry appropriate equipment, and follow any safety guidelines provided by park authorities to ensure a safe and enjoyable experience.

WATER SPORTS (SURFING, KAYAKING, STAND-UP PADDLEBOARDING)

Queensland, with its stunning coastline and waterways, provides abundant opportunities for water sports enthusiasts. Here is some detailed yet concise information about popular water sports in Queensland:

1. Surfing: Queensland boasts some world-class surf breaks along its coastline, attracting surfers of all levels. The Gold Coast is particularly renowned for its consistent waves, with famous breaks like Snapper Rocks, Burleigh Heads, and Kirra. Further north, the Sunshine Coast offers excellent surf spots such as Noosa Heads and Coolum Beach. Experienced surfers often seek out the powerful breaks at places like the legendary Superbank in Coolangatta.

2. Kayaking: With its numerous rivers, lakes, and estuaries, Queensland provides fantastic opportunities for kayaking. The Noosa Everglades, located in the Great Sandy National Park, is a popular kayaking destination. Paddling through its pristine waters surrounded by lush rainforest offers a serene and unforgettable experience. Additionally, the Brisbane River, Moreton Bay, and various coastal regions provide scenic spots for kayaking enthusiasts.

3. Stand-Up Paddleboarding (SUP): Stand-Up Paddleboarding has gained immense popularity in Queensland due to its versatility and accessibility. SUP allows participants to explore calm waterways, ride waves, and even engage in yoga or fitness sessions on the water. Noosa River, Southport Broadwater, and the tranquil water bodies of the Whitsunday Islands are perfect locations for SUP adventures.

4. Great Barrier Reef Snorkeling: While snorkelling is not strictly a water sport, it provides an incredible opportunity to explore the underwater wonders of the Great Barrier Reef. Numerous tour operators in Queensland offer snorkelling trips to the reef, allowing visitors to witness the vibrant coral gardens and encounter a diverse array of marine life, including tropical fish, turtles, and colourful coral formations.

5. Jet Skiing: For those seeking an adrenaline rush, jet skiing is a thrilling water sport in Queensland. With vast stretches of coastline and open waters, there are ample locations to rent jet skis and enjoy high-speed rides. The Gold Coast Broadwater,

Moreton Bay, and the Whitsunday Islands are popular spots for jet skiing adventures.

6. Kiteboarding and Windsurfing: Queensland's breezy coastal conditions make it ideal for kiteboarding and windsurfing. Places like Airlie Beach, Mission Beach, and the Great Sandy Strait provide ample space and consistent winds for these exhilarating water sports. Lessons and equipment rentals are available for beginners and experienced riders alike.

It's important to prioritise safety when engaging in water sports. Be aware of local conditions, follow safety guidelines, wear appropriate gear, and, if necessary, take lessons from qualified instructors to enhance your skills and ensure a safe and enjoyable experience.

SKYDIVING, BUNGEE JUMPING, AND HOT AIR BALLOONING

Queensland offers thrilling adventures for adrenaline junkies with its skydiving, bungee jumping, and hot air ballooning experiences. Here is some detailed yet concise information about each activity:

1. Skydiving: Skydiving in Queensland provides a unique opportunity to experience the exhilaration of freefall and witness stunning aerial views. Popular skydiving locations include the Gold Coast, Cairns, and Mission Beach. Tandem skydiving is the most common option, where you jump in tandem with an experienced instructor who guides you throughout the entire experience. You'll enjoy a thrilling freefall followed by a peaceful parachute descent, taking in breathtaking coastal or rainforest scenery.

2. Bungee Jumping: Bungee jumping enthusiasts can find heart-pumping experiences in Queensland as well. The AJ Hackett Bungy site in

Cairns offers the opportunity to leap from a 50-metre (164-foot) tower above a rainforest-fringed pool. The adrenaline rush of the jump and the surrounding lush scenery combine to create an unforgettable experience. Safety is paramount, and professional staff ensure all equipment and procedures meet high standards.

3. Hot Air Ballooning: Hot air ballooning provides a serene and awe-inspiring adventure, allowing you to float peacefully over Queensland's picturesque landscapes. The Scenic Rim region, including areas near Brisbane and the Gold Coast, is popular for hot air ballooning. As the balloon gently ascends, you'll enjoy panoramic views of rolling hills, vineyards, and even glimpses of the coast. It's an ideal way to witness stunning sunrises and take in the natural beauty of the region.

Safety Considerations: When participating in these activities, it's crucial to prioritise safety. Operators should be licensed, certified, and have a strong safety record. They provide safety equipment, conduct thorough briefings, and adhere to strict protocols to ensure your well-being throughout the experience.

Age and Health Requirements: Each activity may have age and health restrictions. Make sure to check the specific requirements set by the operators to ensure you meet the criteria for participation.

Booking and Availability: It's advisable to book these activities in advance, especially during peak seasons, to secure your spot. Weather conditions can also impact availability, so be prepared for potential schedule changes due to inclement weather.

These adrenaline-pumping activities offer a unique way to explore Queensland's natural beauty and create unforgettable memories. Whether you choose skydiving, bungee jumping, or hot air ballooning, each experience promises an exhilarating adventure that showcases the stunning landscapes of this beautiful state.

4WD AND OFF-ROAD ADVENTURES

Queensland's diverse landscapes and rugged terrains make it an ideal destination for 4WD and off-road adventures. Here is some detailed yet concise information about 4WD and off-road adventures in Queensland:

1. Fraser Island: Fraser Island, located off the coast of Hervey Bay, is the largest sand island in the world and a haven for 4WD enthusiasts. With designated driving tracks that wind through sandy beaches, rainforests, and freshwater lakes, Fraser Island offers a unique off-road experience. Highlights include the iconic Seventy-Five Mile Beach, the beautiful Lake McKenzie, and the challenging tracks of the inland rainforest.

2. Cape York Peninsula: The Cape York Peninsula in Far North Queensland is an off-road adventurer's paradise. It offers rugged terrain, river crossings, and challenging tracks that lead to the northernmost point of mainland Australia, Cape

York. The Old Telegraph Track is a famous 4WD route known for its water crossings and challenging obstacles, while the Cape Melville National Park showcases stunning coastal landscapes.

3. Moreton Island: Moreton Island, located off the coast of Brisbane, provides a mix of sand tracks, coastal driving, and off-road adventures. You can explore the island's scenic sand dunes, visit the Tangalooma Wrecks, and drive along the expansive beaches. The Big Sandhills and the Blue Lagoon are popular spots for sandboarding and swimming.

4. Glass House Mountains: The Glass House Mountains, situated north of Brisbane, offer a combination of off-road trails and stunning volcanic peaks. With tracks like the Conondale Range Great Walk and the Mount Mee Forest Reserve, you can enjoy scenic drives through lush forests and explore the diverse landscape of the region.

5. Daintree Rainforest: The Daintree Rainforest, located in Far North Queensland, provides opportunities for 4WD exploration on its remote tracks. The famous Bloomfield Track is a challenging yet rewarding route that winds through dense rainforest, creek crossings, and stunning coastal vistas. It connects Cape Tribulation with Cooktown and offers an off-road adventure amidst ancient natural wonders.

Safety and Permits: It's essential to have a suitable 4WD vehicle, be experienced in off-road driving, and carry necessary recovery equipment. Some areas may require permits or have restricted access, so it's important to check local regulations and obtain any required permits beforehand.

Environmental Considerations: When engaging in off-road adventures, it's crucial to respect the environment and minimise your impact. Stick to designated tracks, avoid damaging vegetation, and follow any guidelines or regulations provided by local authorities.

Queensland's 4WD and off-road adventures offer the opportunity to explore stunning landscapes, tackle challenging terrains, and experience the thrill of off-road driving. It's an exciting way to discover the state's diverse natural beauty and create unforgettable memories.

NATIONAL PARKS AND NATURAL WONDERS

LAMINGTON NATIONAL PARK

Lamington National Park is a renowned national park located in Queensland, Australia. It is part of the Gondwana Rainforests of Australia World Heritage Area and is recognized for its exceptional biodiversity and stunning natural landscapes. Here is some detailed yet concise information about Lamington National Park:

1. Location: Lamington National Park is situated on the Lamington Plateau of the McPherson Range, on the border between Queensland and New South Wales, approximately 85 kilometres (53 miles) south of Brisbane, the capital city of Queensland.

2. Size: The national park covers an area of approximately 206 square kilometres (80 square miles).

3. Rainforest Heritage: Lamington National Park forms a significant part of the Gondwana Rainforests of Australia, which is a UNESCO World Heritage-listed site. This recognition highlights the park's immense ecological value and ancient rainforest ecosystems.

4. Flora and Fauna: The park boasts incredible biodiversity, with lush rainforests, cascading waterfalls, and diverse plant and animal species. It is home to over 1,000 plant species, including ancient Antarctic beech trees, along with numerous ferns, orchids, and towering eucalyptus trees. Wildlife enthusiasts can spot various animals like koalas, wallabies, pademelons, and over 190 bird species, including the vibrant Regent Bowerbird and Albert's Lyrebird.

5. Walks and Hikes: Lamington National Park offers an extensive network of walking trails and hiking routes, catering to different fitness levels and interests. The most famous trek is the 21-kilometre (13-mile) Albert River Circuit, also known as the Border Track, which spans between Queensland and New South Wales. The walk

provides breathtaking vistas, pristine rainforest experiences, and a chance to explore the unique border region.

6. Waterfalls and Lookouts: The park features several picturesque waterfalls and panoramic lookout points that offer awe-inspiring views. Some notable attractions include the breathtaking Moran Falls, Purling Brook Falls with its suspended bridge, and the aptly named Best of All Lookout, which provides sweeping vistas of the surrounding valleys and coastline.

7. Accommodation: Visitors can choose from a range of accommodation options within or near the park, including the historic O'Reilly's Rainforest Retreat, which offers lodges, cabins, and camping facilities. The retreat also hosts guided tours, bird feeding sessions, and the chance to spot nocturnal wildlife on a glowworm tour.

8. Visitor Facilities: Lamington National Park provides visitor facilities such as picnic areas, barbecue spots, and interpretive displays to enhance the visitor experience. It is advisable to

carry sufficient water, snacks, and appropriate clothing while exploring the park's trails.

Lamington National Park is a haven for nature lovers, offering a serene and captivating environment to explore the wonders of Queensland's ancient rainforests.

DAINTREE RAINFOREST AND WET TROPICS WORLD HERITAGE AREA

Daintree Rainforest is a unique and ecologically significant tropical rainforest located in Queensland, Australia. It is part of the larger Wet Tropics World Heritage Area. Here is some detailed yet concise information about the Daintree Rainforest and the Wet Tropics World Heritage Area:

1. Location: The Daintree Rainforest is situated in Far North Queensland, approximately 110

kilometres (68 miles) north of Cairns, a popular tourist destination in Australia. It spans an area of about 1,200 square kilometres (460 square miles).

2. Ancient Rainforest: The Daintree Rainforest is considered one of the oldest rainforests in the world, with its origins dating back over 180 million years. It is a living remnant of the ancient Gondwana Rainforests, and its preservation provides a glimpse into the planet's evolutionary past.

3. Biodiversity Hotspot: The Daintree Rainforest is renowned for its remarkable biodiversity, harbouring an astonishing array of plant and animal species. It is home to an estimated 3,000 plant species, including rare and endangered species like the iconic Daintree fan palm, primitive flowering plants, and a variety of orchids. The rainforest also supports diverse wildlife, including cassowaries, tree kangaroos, flying foxes, and countless bird species.

4. Unique Ecosystems: The rainforest comprises a complex web of ecosystems, encompassing

lowland rainforest, upland cloud forests, mangrove swamps, and freshwater streams. The intricate balance between these ecosystems provides crucial habitat for a multitude of species and contributes to the region's overall ecological integrity.

5. Indigenous Cultural Significance: The Daintree Rainforest holds great cultural significance for the local Indigenous peoples, particularly the Kuku Yalanji people. They have inhabited the region for thousands of years and consider the rainforest a living cultural landscape, rich in traditional knowledge and spiritual connections.

6. Cape Tribulation: Within the Daintree Rainforest, you'll find Cape Tribulation, where the rainforest meets the stunning coastline. This picturesque area is named after the trials faced by Captain James Cook when his ship, the HMS Endeavour, ran aground on the nearby Great Barrier Reef. Cape Tribulation offers beautiful beaches, mangrove boardwalks, and opportunities for reef snorkelling and wildlife cruises.

7. Wet Tropics World Heritage Area: The Daintree Rainforest is part of the Wet Tropics World Heritage Area, a region recognized by UNESCO for its exceptional natural and cultural values. This World Heritage Area covers approximately 8,940 square kilometres (3,450 square miles) and encompasses not only the Daintree Rainforest but also other diverse ecosystems and landscapes.

8. Conservation and Tourism: The conservation of the Daintree Rainforest and the Wet Tropics World Heritage Area is a priority, with efforts focused on preserving its unique biodiversity and supporting sustainable tourism. Visitors can explore the rainforest through guided walks, 4WD tours, river cruises, and even zip-lining adventures, all while adhering to responsible and eco-friendly practices.

The Daintree Rainforest and the Wet Tropics World Heritage Area offer an immersive and awe-inspiring experience, allowing visitors to witness the beauty and ecological significance of one of Australia's most exceptional natural wonders.

GREAT SANDY NATIONAL PARK AND FRASER ISLAND

Great Sandy National Park is a stunning coastal national park located in Queensland, Australia. It is renowned for encompassing Fraser Island, the largest sand island in the world. Here is some detailed yet concise information about Great Sandy National Park and Fraser Island:

1. Location: Great Sandy National Park is situated on the southeastern coast of Queensland, approximately 250 kilometres (155 miles) north of Brisbane. It spans a vast area of approximately 220,000 hectares (543,000 acres).

2. Fraser Island: The centrepiece of Great Sandy National Park is Fraser Island, a UNESCO World Heritage site and a popular tourist destination. Spanning over 1,840 square kilometres (710 square miles), Fraser Island is known for its pristine beaches, crystal-clear freshwater lakes, towering sand dunes, and lush rainforests.

3. Sand Island Wonder: Fraser Island is entirely composed of sand and is the largest sand island globally, stretching approximately 123 kilometres (76 miles) in length. It is a unique and fragile ecosystem that has evolved over thousands of years, providing a habitat for diverse plant and animal species.

4. Unique Ecosystems: Fraser Island showcases a variety of ecosystems, including subtropical rainforests, tall eucalyptus forests, mangrove forests, and perched freshwater lakes. The island's immense biodiversity is home to several endemic and endangered species, such as the Fraser Island dingo, Eastern curlew, and acid frogs.

5. Natural Wonders: Fraser Island offers a plethora of natural attractions. Visitors can explore the stunning Lake McKenzie, a picturesque freshwater lake with crystal-clear turquoise waters, or swim in the Champagne Pools, natural rock pools formed by crashing waves. The island is also famous for its iconic landmark, the Maheno Shipwreck, which rests on the shore and provides a glimpse into the island's maritime history.

6. 4WD Adventure: Due to the sandy terrain, the primary mode of transportation on Fraser Island is 4WD vehicles. Visitors can embark on exhilarating 4WD adventures along designated tracks that traverse the island, providing access to its various attractions, including the famous Seventy-Five Mile Beach, the world's longest beach highway.

7. Camping and Accommodation: Great Sandy National Park offers a range of camping options on Fraser Island, with numerous campgrounds available. Visitors can also find accommodation in resorts, lodges, and holiday houses scattered across the island, catering to different preferences and budgets.

8. Conservation and Protection: Great Sandy National Park and Fraser Island are protected areas, with conservation efforts aimed at preserving their unique ecosystems and cultural heritage. Visitors are encouraged to follow responsible tourism practices, including respecting wildlife, taking only photographs, and leaving no trace behind.

Great Sandy National Park and Fraser Island provide an extraordinary blend of natural wonders, offering a remarkable combination of stunning landscapes, diverse ecosystems, and cultural significance. It is a must-visit destination for nature lovers and adventure seekers alike.

GIRRINGUN NATIONAL PARK AND WALLAMAN FALLS

Girringun National Park is a picturesque national park located in Queensland, Australia. It is known for its magnificent centrepiece, Wallaman Falls, which is the tallest single-drop waterfall in Australia. Here is some detailed yet concise information about Girringun National Park and Wallaman Falls:

1. Location: Girringun National Park is situated in North Queensland, approximately 210 kilometres (130 miles) northwest of Townsville. It covers an

area of about 87,000 hectares (215,000 acres) and is part of the Wet Tropics World Heritage Area.

2. Wallaman Falls: The highlight of Girringun National Park is Wallaman Falls, a natural wonder that plunges 268 metres (879 feet) from an escarpment into a picturesque gorge below. It is Australia's highest single-drop waterfall and is renowned for its impressive beauty and raw power.

3. Spectacular Scenery: The area surrounding Wallaman Falls is characterised by stunning landscapes, with rugged cliffs, lush rainforests, and cascading streams. The viewing platform at the falls provides a breathtaking vantage point to witness the sheer grandeur and misty spray of the waterfall.

4. Biodiversity Hotspot: Girringun National Park is rich in biodiversity and is home to a diverse range of plant and animal species. The park protects a significant portion of the Wet Tropics Rainforest, which is recognized for its exceptional ecological value. Visitors can encounter unique flora,

including ancient trees, orchids, and a variety of bird and animal species.

5. Hiking Trails: The national park offers a network of walking tracks that allow visitors to explore its natural wonders and enjoy the surrounding beauty. The iconic Thorsborne Trail is a challenging multi-day hike that traverses the rugged terrain of the park and offers spectacular views of Wallaman Falls and the Herbert River.

6. Cultural Significance: Girringun National Park has significant cultural value for the Traditional Owners, the Warrgamay Gan and Jirrbal Aboriginal people. The area holds spiritual importance, and visitors are encouraged to respect the land, its history, and the cultural heritage of the Indigenous communities.

7. Visitor Facilities: The park provides basic visitor facilities, including picnic areas, toilets, and a camping area near the falls. It is advisable to check for any park alerts or closures before planning a visit and to carry necessary supplies, including water, food, and appropriate hiking gear.

8. Conservation and Management: Girringun National Park is managed collaboratively by the Queensland Government and the Traditional Owners to preserve its natural and cultural values. Efforts are focused on sustainable tourism practices, conservation initiatives, and ongoing research to protect the park's unique ecosystems.

Girringun National Park and Wallaman Falls offer a mesmerising natural experience, allowing visitors to witness the power and beauty of Australia's tallest waterfall, surrounded by pristine rainforests and captivating landscapes.

CARNARVON GORGE AND CARNARVON NATIONAL PARK

Carnarvon Gorge is a breathtaking natural attraction located within Carnarvon National Park in Queensland, Australia. It is known for its stunning sandstone cliffs, ancient Aboriginal rock art, and picturesque hiking trails. Here is some detailed yet concise information about Carnarvon Gorge and Carnarvon National Park:

1. Location: Carnarvon Gorge is situated in central Queensland, approximately 600 kilometres (370 miles) northwest of Brisbane. It is part of Carnarvon National Park, which covers an area of about 298,000 hectares (736,000 acres).

2. Sandstone Splendor: The main highlight of Carnarvon National Park is Carnarvon Gorge, a deep and rugged gorge carved out by Carnarvon Creek. The gorge is renowned for its towering sandstone cliffs, scenic waterholes, and lush vegetation, creating a stunning natural backdrop.

3. Aboriginal Heritage: Carnarvon Gorge holds significant cultural importance for the Traditional Owners, the Bidjara and Karingbal Aboriginal people. The area contains a wealth of Aboriginal rock art, some of which dates back thousands of years. These artworks provide a glimpse into the rich cultural history and spiritual significance of the region.

4. Hiking and Nature Trails: The national park offers a network of well-maintained hiking trails that allow visitors to explore the natural wonders of Carnarvon Gorge. The most popular walk is the Carnarvon Gorge Main Track, a 9-kilometre (5.6-mile) trail that meanders along the creek, passing by impressive rock formations, vibrant flora, and several notable sites, including the Moss Garden and Amphitheatre.

5. Wildlife and Flora: Carnarvon National Park is teeming with diverse wildlife and plant species. Visitors may encounter wallabies, kangaroos, platypus, and a variety of bird species, including the colourful king parrot and the elusive lyrebird. The park's vegetation ranges from subtropical rainforest to eucalypt woodlands, with an abundance of ferns, cycads, and wildflowers.

6. Natural Attractions: Carnarvon Gorge boasts several natural attractions that add to its allure. These include the Moss Garden, a serene oasis covered in lush green mosses and ferns, and the Amphitheatre, a towering sandstone gorge with

remarkable acoustics that make it a popular spot for performances and musical events.

7. Camping and Facilities: Carnarvon National Park provides camping facilities for visitors, including a campground near the gorge. Additionally, there is a visitor centre at the park entrance where visitors can obtain information, maps, and permits.

8. Conservation and Protection: Carnarvon National Park is managed by the Queensland Government to protect its unique natural and cultural values. Conservation efforts focus on preserving the fragile ecosystem, promoting sustainable tourism practices, and educating visitors about the park's significance.

Carnarvon Gorge and Carnarvon National Park offer a captivating blend of natural beauty, cultural heritage, and outdoor adventure. It is a must-visit destination for hikers, nature enthusiasts, and those seeking a profound connection with Queensland's natural wonders.

EVENTS AND FESTIVALS
IN QUEENSLAND

BRISBANE FESTIVAL

The Brisbane Festival is an annual multi-disciplinary arts festival held in Brisbane, the capital city of Queensland, Australia. It showcases a diverse range of performances and events, including music, dance, theatre, visual arts, circus, and more. The festival aims to celebrate and promote the cultural vibrancy of the city and provide a platform for local, national, and international artists to showcase their work.

The festival usually takes place over several weeks, spanning the months of September and October. It features a packed program of events that are held at various venues across Brisbane, including theatres, outdoor spaces, galleries, and cultural centres. The festival attracts a wide audience, from local residents to visitors from around Australia and beyond.

The Brisbane Festival offers a mix of ticketed and free events, ensuring accessibility to a broad range of audiences. It presents both large-scale productions and intimate performances, catering to different artistic tastes and interests. The program includes performances by renowned artists, emerging talents, and collaborations between local and international creatives.

In addition to performances, the festival often incorporates interactive installations, public art displays, and community engagement initiatives. These activities aim to foster participation, dialogue, and a sense of community among festival attendees.

The festival has become a significant cultural event in Brisbane, attracting thousands of people each year. It contributes to the city's cultural and economic growth by showcasing the artistic talent of the region and generating tourism and visitor expenditure.

Overall, the Brisbane Festival is a vibrant celebration of arts and culture, providing a platform for artists and audiences to engage, explore, and be inspired by a diverse range of artistic expressions.

GOLD COAST COMMONWEALTH GAMES

The Gold Coast Commonwealth Games was a major international sporting event held on the Gold Coast in Queensland, Australia, from April 4 to April 15, 2018. It was the fifth time Australia hosted the Commonwealth Games and the first time the event was held in Queensland.

The Commonwealth Games is a multi-sport event that brings together athletes from countries and territories that are members of the Commonwealth. The Gold Coast Games featured 71 nations and territories, with approximately 4,400 athletes competing across 18 sports and 7 para-sports.

The event encompassed a wide range of sporting disciplines, including athletics, swimming, cycling, gymnastics, netball, rugby sevens, and more. The competitions took place at various venues across the Gold Coast, as well as in Brisbane, Cairns, and Townsville.

The Gold Coast Games aimed to showcase the region's natural beauty and hospitality while providing world-class sporting facilities and infrastructure. The event left a lasting legacy for the Gold Coast and Queensland, including the development of new sporting facilities, upgraded transport systems, and improved community and recreational spaces.

In addition to the sporting events, the Gold Coast Commonwealth Games also included a vibrant cultural program known as Festival 2018. This program featured live performances, art installations, exhibitions, and community events, offering a diverse range of cultural experiences for visitors and locals alike.

The Games were considered a great success, with athletes delivering outstanding performances and breaking numerous records. The event was praised for its organisation, hospitality, and the enthusiastic support of the local community.

The Gold Coast Commonwealth Games provided an opportunity for Queensland to showcase its capabilities as a host for major international events and contributed to the growth of tourism and the economy in the region. It left a lasting legacy of improved infrastructure, increased sporting participation, and a heightened sense of community pride.

CAIRNS INDIGENOUS ART FAIR

The Cairns Indigenous Art Fair (CIAF) is an annual event held in Cairns, Queensland, Australia, that celebrates and promotes the rich artistic and cultural heritage of Indigenous peoples from Queensland and beyond. The fair showcases a diverse range of Indigenous art, including traditional and contemporary works, across various mediums such as painting, sculpture, textiles, weaving, and more.

The CIAF provides a platform for Indigenous artists to exhibit and sell their artwork directly to the public and collectors. It aims to support and empower Indigenous artists, fostering economic opportunities and cultural exchange. The fair also promotes cultural awareness and understanding by sharing stories, traditions, and knowledge through art.

In addition to the art exhibition and sales, the CIAF offers a dynamic program of events and activities. These include dance performances, music concerts, workshops, cultural talks, fashion shows, and culinary experiences featuring Indigenous cuisine. The fair creates a vibrant and immersive atmosphere, engaging visitors in the richness of Indigenous culture.

The CIAF is renowned for its commitment to ethical and sustainable practices, ensuring artists receive fair compensation for their work. It also prioritises cultural integrity, providing a respectful and inclusive platform for Indigenous voices and perspectives.

The fair attracts a diverse audience, including art enthusiasts, collectors, tourists, and members of the local community. It has gained national and international recognition as a leading Indigenous art event, contributing to the cultural landscape of Queensland and Australia as a whole.

The Cairns Indigenous Art Fair plays a vital role in promoting and preserving Indigenous art and culture, fostering economic opportunities for Indigenous artists, and building bridges of understanding between Indigenous and non-Indigenous communities. It serves as a significant platform for the empowerment and celebration of Indigenous artistic talent.

NOOSA FOOD AND WINE FESTIVAL

The Noosa Food and Wine Festival is an annual culinary event held in Noosa, a coastal town in Queensland, Australia. It showcases the region's vibrant food and wine scene, featuring a diverse range of culinary experiences, from gourmet meals prepared by renowned chefs to wine tastings, cooking demonstrations, and more.

The festival typically takes place over several days, offering attendees the opportunity to indulge in a variety of food and wine-related activities. It brings together acclaimed chefs, winemakers, and food enthusiasts from around the country and internationally, creating a dynamic and engaging atmosphere.

The Noosa Food and Wine Festival showcases the local produce, flavours, and culinary talent of the region. It features cooking demonstrations and masterclasses by top chefs, providing insights into their techniques and philosophies. Visitors can sample delicious dishes created by renowned chefs at various events, including long lunches, degustation dinners, and food stalls.

The festival also highlights the region's wine and beverage industry, offering tastings and pairing sessions with local wines, craft beers, and spirits. Attendees have the opportunity to meet winemakers and learn about the region's viticulture and production processes.

In addition to the culinary experiences, the Noosa Food and Wine Festival often includes live entertainment, music performances, and cultural activities, adding to the festive atmosphere. The event takes advantage of Noosa's natural beauty, with some events held on the beach or in picturesque outdoor settings.

The Noosa Food and Wine Festival attracts a diverse audience, including food lovers, wine connoisseurs, and those seeking a memorable culinary experience. It contributes to the local economy and tourism, showcasing Noosa as a premier food and wine destination.

Overall, the Noosa Food and Wine Festival celebrates the gastronomic delights of the region, highlighting the talents of chefs, winemakers, and producers while offering an enjoyable and immersive experience for attendees.

WOODFORD FOLK FESTIVAL

The Woodford Folk Festival is an annual music and cultural festival held in Woodford, Queensland, Australia. It is one of the largest folk festivals in the southern hemisphere, attracting tens of thousands of attendees from around the country and the world.

The festival takes place over six days, usually from December 27 to January 1, creating a vibrant and inclusive community atmosphere. It showcases a diverse range of music genres, including folk, world music, blues, jazz, rock, and more. The festival stages feature performances by both renowned artists and emerging talents, with a strong emphasis on live music.

In addition to the music program, the Woodford Folk Festival offers a rich cultural experience through various art forms. This includes theatre performances, dance workshops, circus acts, street performances, visual arts displays, and storytelling sessions. Attendees can immerse themselves in a wide range of artistic expressions and participate in interactive activities.

The festival grounds are transformed into a bustling village, with numerous venues, stalls, and food vendors. The atmosphere is vibrant and family-friendly, with a dedicated children's program offering activities and performances tailored to young festival-goers.

Woodford Folk Festival also places a strong emphasis on sustainability and environmental consciousness. It promotes eco-friendly practices, including waste reduction, recycling, and sustainable energy initiatives. The festival aims to inspire and educate attendees about environmental stewardship and social responsibility.

The Woodford Folk Festival is renowned for its inclusive and welcoming atmosphere. It encourages participation and engagement from attendees, fostering a sense of community and cultural exchange. The festival provides a platform for artists, musicians, and performers to showcase their talents, and it has become a significant event in Queensland's cultural calendar.

Overall, the Woodford Folk Festival offers a unique and immersive experience, celebrating music, arts, and culture while promoting sustainability and community engagement. It is a cherished event for both performers and attendees, creating lasting memories and fostering connections in a vibrant and diverse setting.

SHOPPING AND SOUVENIRS

POPULAR SHOPPING DESTINATIONS IN QUEENSLAND

Queensland, Australia, offers a variety of popular shopping destinations that cater to different interests and preferences. Here are some of the top shopping destinations in Queensland:

1. Queen Street Mall (Brisbane): Located in the heart of Brisbane's CBD, Queen Street Mall is a vibrant shopping precinct that features over 700 retailers, including major department stores, boutique shops, and international brands. It is a pedestrian-only mall and a hub for fashion, accessories, electronics, and more.

2. Pacific Fair Shopping Centre (Gold Coast): Situated in Broadbeach, Pacific Fair is one of the largest shopping centres in Queensland. It boasts

over 400 specialty stores, high-end fashion boutiques, dining options, and entertainment facilities. The centre recently underwent a major redevelopment, offering a modern and luxurious shopping experience.

3. Harbour Town Outlet Shopping Centre (Gold Coast): Located in Biggera Waters, Harbour Town is a popular destination for bargain hunters. It features over 240 outlet stores offering discounted prices on fashion, accessories, homeware, and more. Visitors can find both local and international brands at reduced prices.

4. Noosa Heads: Noosa Heads, a coastal town on the Sunshine Coast, is renowned for its boutique shopping scene. Hastings Street is the main shopping hub, offering an array of fashion boutiques, gift shops, art galleries, and upscale stores. Visitors can enjoy a relaxed shopping experience while exploring the beautiful surroundings.

5. Cairns Central Shopping Centre (Cairns): Cairns Central is the largest shopping centre in Far North

Queensland. It houses a wide range of retailers, including major department stores, fashion outlets, beauty salons, and electronics shops. The centre also features a cinema complex and a variety of dining options.

6. Indooroopilly Shopping Centre (Brisbane): Located in the western suburbs of Brisbane, Indooroopilly Shopping Centre is a popular destination for fashion, accessories, and homewares. With over 360 specialty stores, including high-end brands and department stores, it caters to a diverse range of shopping needs.

7. Robina Town Centre (Gold Coast): Situated in Robina, this expansive shopping centre offers over 400 stores spread across two levels. Robina Town Centre features a mix of major retailers, boutique shops, and entertainment options. The centre's modern design and open-air atmosphere make it a popular choice for locals and tourists alike.

These are just a few examples of the popular shopping destinations in Queensland. The state offers a wide range of options for every shopper, from luxury boutiques and department stores to outlet shopping centres and unique local markets.

INDIGENOUS ART AND CRAFTS

Indigenous art and crafts play a significant role in the cultural heritage of Queensland, Australia. The Aboriginal and Torres Strait Islander peoples of Queensland have a rich artistic tradition that encompasses a wide range of mediums and styles. Here is some detailed yet concise information about Indigenous art and crafts in Queensland:

1. Traditional Art Forms: Indigenous artists in Queensland have a deep connection to their ancestral lands and express their cultural heritage through various art forms. These include dot painting, bark painting, rock art, sand art, weaving, wood carving, and ceramics. Each art form carries symbolic meanings, stories, and spiritual significance that reflect the Indigenous peoples' connection to the land, animals, and Dreamtime mythology.

2. Cultural Significance: Indigenous art and crafts in Queensland hold immense cultural and historical significance. They serve as a means of passing down traditional knowledge, preserving cultural practices, and telling stories of the Dreaming, which refers to the creation period in Aboriginal and Torres Strait Islander cultures. Art is also a form of cultural expression, activism, and a way to assert Indigenous identity and rights.

3. Art Centers and Galleries: Throughout Queensland, there are numerous art centres and galleries that support and showcase Indigenous art. These institutions provide platforms for Indigenous artists to exhibit and sell their works. Some prominent examples include the Cairns Indigenous Art Fair, Gab Titui Cultural Centre on Thursday Island, and the State Library of Queensland's kuril dhagun Indigenous space in Brisbane.

4. Contemporary Indigenous Art: Indigenous art in Queensland has evolved and embraced contemporary styles and techniques. Many artists fuse traditional methods with contemporary

mediums like acrylic paints, digital art, and sculpture. Contemporary Indigenous artists often explore themes of identity, social issues, land rights, and cultural resilience, showcasing the ongoing vitality and adaptability of Indigenous art in Queensland.

5. Indigenous Crafts and Souvenirs: Visitors to Queensland can find a diverse range of Indigenous crafts and souvenirs, both in dedicated Indigenous art galleries and cultural centres, as well as in local markets and souvenir shops. These crafts include handwoven baskets, traditional jewellery, didgeridoos, boomerangs, paintings, sculptures, and prints. It is important to ensure that the purchase of Indigenous art and crafts supports authentic Indigenous artists and respects their intellectual and cultural property rights.

Indigenous art and crafts in Queensland are not only visually stunning but also serve as a powerful means of cultural preservation, storytelling, and celebration. They provide opportunities for cross-cultural exchange, appreciation, and understanding, allowing visitors to connect with the rich cultural heritage of Queensland's Aboriginal and Torres Strait Islander peoples.

LOCAL MARKETS AND BOUTIQUES

Queensland, Australia, is home to a vibrant array of local markets and boutiques, offering unique shopping experiences and a chance to support local businesses. Here is some detailed yet concise information about local markets and boutiques in Queensland:

1. Eumundi Markets (Sunshine Coast): The Eumundi Markets, located in the town of Eumundi, are one of Queensland's most renowned markets. Operating every Wednesday and Saturday, the market showcases a wide range of locally made products, including arts and crafts, fashion, homewares, and fresh produce. It is a bustling hub for artisans, designers, and food vendors, attracting both locals and tourists alike.

2. Jan Powers Farmers Markets (Brisbane): Jan Powers Farmers Markets are held at various locations throughout Brisbane, including the Powerhouse at New Farm, Manly, and Mitchelton. These markets specialise in fresh, locally sourced produce, including fruits, vegetables, meats, cheeses, and baked goods. They offer an opportunity to support local farmers and producers while enjoying the vibrant atmosphere.

3. Noosa Farmers Market (Sunshine Coast): The Noosa Farmers Market, held every Sunday, showcases the best of local produce, gourmet foods, and artisan products. Visitors can browse through a wide range of stalls offering fresh fruits and vegetables, organic products, baked goods, locally made cheeses, and more. The market is a popular spot for food lovers and those seeking high-quality local ingredients.

4. James Street (Brisbane): Located in the trendy suburb of Fortitude Valley, James Street is a premier destination for boutique shopping. The street is lined with a curated selection of high-end fashion boutiques, design stores, art galleries, and

stylish cafes. It is known for its unique blend of local and international brands, making it a go-to spot for fashion-forward individuals.

5. Port Douglas Sunday Market (Far North Queensland): The Port Douglas Sunday Market is held on the waterfront at Anzac Park and showcases an eclectic mix of local arts, crafts, and produce. Visitors can explore stalls offering handmade jewellery, artworks, clothing, skincare products, and tropical fruits. The market's relaxed tropical setting adds to its charm.

6. Currumbin Community Markets (Gold Coast): The Currumbin Community Markets, held every Thursday at the Currumbin Wildlife Sanctuary, offer a diverse range of locally made products and fresh produce. Visitors can discover unique arts and crafts, fashion items, and gourmet food while enjoying the beautiful surroundings of the wildlife sanctuary.

7. Paddington Antique Centre (Brisbane): Located in the inner-city suburb of Paddington, the Paddington Antique Centre is a treasure trove for

antique enthusiasts. The centre features multiple levels of stalls offering a wide range of antique furniture, vintage clothing, retro collectibles, and unique home decor items. It is a must-visit destination for those with a passion for timeless pieces.

These local markets and boutiques in Queensland provide opportunities to explore local craftsmanship, support small businesses, and find one-of-a-kind products. Whether it's fresh produce, artisanal goods, or unique vintage finds, these shopping destinations offer a delightful experience for residents and visitors alike.

UNIQUE QUEENSLAND SOUVENIRS

Queensland, Australia, offers a variety of unique souvenirs that capture the essence of the state's culture, natural beauty, and local traditions. Here is some detailed yet concise information about unique Queensland souvenirs:

1. Opals: Queensland is known for its opal deposits, and opal jewellery makes for a stunning and distinctive souvenir. Opals come in various colours and can be found in earrings, pendants, rings, and bracelets. Look for certified opals from reputable jewellers to ensure their authenticity.

2. Indigenous Art and Crafts: Indigenous art and crafts reflect the rich cultural heritage of Queensland's Aboriginal and Torres Strait Islander peoples. Handwoven baskets, traditional paintings, didgeridoos, boomerangs, and indigenous-designed clothing are among the unique souvenirs that offer a connection to the state's Indigenous traditions.

3. Macadamia Nuts: Queensland is a major producer of macadamia nuts, known for their rich flavour and buttery texture. Purchase packages of roasted or chocolate-covered macadamia nuts as a tasty souvenir to bring back home. Look for brands that source their macadamias locally for an authentic taste.

4. Tim Tam Biscuits: Tim Tam biscuits are an iconic Australian treat that makes for a delicious souvenir. These chocolate-coated biscuits have a unique texture and come in various flavours. Look for limited-edition or specialty flavours that are exclusive to Australia.

5. Australia-themed Clothing and Accessories: Queensland offers a wide range of Australia-themed clothing and accessories that make for fun and practical souvenirs. T-shirts, hats, and tote bags featuring kangaroos, koalas, and other iconic Australian animals are popular choices. Look for locally designed and made items for an authentic touch.

6. Great Barrier Reef-inspired Items: The Great Barrier Reef is a UNESCO World Heritage Site and one of Queensland's most famous natural wonders. Look for souvenirs that are inspired by the reef, such as coral-themed jewellery, reef-inspired artwork, or eco-friendly sunscreen formulated to protect the reef.

7. Local Art and Photography: Queensland's stunning landscapes and unique wildlife have inspired many talented artists and photographers. Consider purchasing prints, postcards, or calendars featuring local artwork and photography as a beautiful and memorable souvenir.

8. Vintage Surf Memorabilia: Queensland's coastal regions are renowned for their surf culture. Vintage surf memorabilia, such as old surfboards, vintage posters, and surf-inspired clothing, can be unique and nostalgic souvenirs for surf enthusiasts or collectors.

These unique Queensland souvenirs offer a taste of the state's natural wonders, cultural heritage, and local flavours. Whether it's opals, indigenous art, regional treats, or mementos inspired by the surroundings, these souvenirs allow you to bring a piece of Queensland back home with you.

PRACTICAL INFORMATION AND RESOURCES

EMERGENCY CONTACTS AND SAFETY TIPS

Emergency Contacts and Safety Tips in Queensland, Australia:

Emergency Contacts:
1. Emergency Services (Police, Fire, Ambulance): Dial 000
   In case of a life-threatening emergency or immediate danger, dial 000 to reach the appropriate emergency service. Provide clear and concise information about the situation and your location.

2. Queensland Police Service (Non-emergency): 131 444
   Use this number to report non-emergency incidents or seek assistance from the Queensland Police Service.

3. State Emergency Service (SES): 132 500

The SES provides assistance during storms, floods, and other natural disasters. Call this number for non-life-threatening emergency assistance.

4. Poisons Information Centre: 13 11 26

Contact this number for poisoning emergencies, including ingestion, exposure, or bites/stings from dangerous substances, plants, or animals.

5. Lifeline Australia: 13 11 14

Lifeline offers 24/7 crisis support and suicide prevention services. Call this number if you or someone you know needs emotional support.

Safety Tips in Queensland:

1. Extreme Weather:

Queensland is known for its extreme weather conditions. Stay informed about weather forecasts and warnings issued by the Bureau of Meteorology. Prepare an emergency kit with essential supplies, including food, water, medications, and important documents. Follow evacuation orders and stay updated through local news and authorities.

2. Bushfires:

During bushfire season, be vigilant and monitor local fire conditions. Follow advice from local authorities and have a bushfire survival plan in place. Clear vegetation and flammable debris around your property, and ensure you have a reliable water source and firefighting equipment.

3. Floods:

Flooding is common in Queensland, especially during the wet season. Stay informed about flood warnings and avoid crossing flooded roads or waterways. If you live in a flood-prone area, prepare your property by elevating valuables and having sandbags ready. Follow evacuation orders if necessary.

4. Beach Safety:

Queensland's coastline is renowned for its beautiful beaches, but they can present hazards. Swim only at patrolled beaches and between the flags. Follow instructions from lifeguards or surf lifesavers. Be cautious of strong currents, rips, and marine stingers. Stay hydrated, apply sunscreen, and seek shade to avoid heat-related illnesses.

5. Wildlife Awareness:
   Queensland is home to diverse wildlife, including snakes, spiders, and marine creatures. Be cautious when exploring natural areas and avoid touching or approaching unfamiliar animals. If you encounter a snake, keep a safe distance and seek professional assistance for removal if needed. Familiarise yourself with first aid procedures for snake bites.

Remember, these are general safety tips, and it's essential to stay informed about specific safety guidelines and recommendations for your location within Queensland.

TRAVEL AGENCIES AND TOUR OPERATORS

Here are some examples of travel agencies and tour operators in Queensland, Australia:

1. Flight Centre: Flight Centre is a well-known travel agency with multiple branches in Queensland. They offer a wide range of travel services, including flights, accommodation, tours, and holiday packages. They have experienced travel consultants who can assist with planning and booking your travel arrangements.

2. Helloworld Travel: Helloworld Travel is another prominent travel agency operating in Queensland. They provide a comprehensive range of travel services, including flights, accommodation, cruises, tours, and travel insurance. Their consultants have extensive knowledge and can help tailor your travel plans to suit your preferences.

3. Queensland Rail Travel: Queensland Rail Travel specialises in train journeys throughout Queensland and beyond. They offer iconic rail experiences like the Spirit of Queensland, Spirit of the Outback, and the Kuranda Scenic Railway. They provide various packages and itineraries that showcase the natural beauty of Queensland.

4. Adventure Tours Australia: Adventure Tours Australia is a tour operator that focuses on adventure and outdoor activities. They offer a range of guided tours, including hiking, camping, snorkelling, and wildlife experiences. Their tours cater to different levels of fitness and provide opportunities to explore Queensland's stunning landscapes and unique wildlife.

5. Tangalooma Island Resort: Tangalooma Island Resort is a popular tour operator located on Moreton Island, off the coast of Queensland. They offer day trips and longer stays, providing a range of activities such as dolphin feeding, snorkelling, sandboarding, and whale watching (during the whale season). They also have accommodation options for those who wish to stay overnight.

6. Tropical Journeys: Tropical Journeys specialises in tours and experiences in the Great Barrier Reef region. They offer snorkelling and diving trips to the Outer Reef, as well as visits to the Daintree Rainforest and Cape Tribulation. Their tours focus on eco-friendly practices and provide educational insights into the unique ecosystems of the region.

When booking with travel agencies and tour operators, it's important to check their credibility, reviews, and any specific services or destinations they specialise in. Additionally, always ensure they adhere to safety and sustainability standards to have a memorable and responsible travel experience.

USEFUL WEBSITES AND MOBILE APPS

Here are some useful websites and mobile apps for residents and visitors in Queensland, Australia:

Websites:

1. Queensland Government (www.qld.gov.au): The official website of the Queensland Government provides a wealth of information on various topics, including government services, public transportation, health and safety, education, and tourism. It's a valuable resource for accessing government forms, permits, and regulations.

2. Bureau of Meteorology (www.bom.gov.au): The Bureau of Meteorology website offers up-to-date weather forecasts, warnings, and radar imagery for different regions of Queensland. It's essential for staying informed about weather conditions, especially during severe weather events.

3. TransLink (translink.com.au): TransLink is Queensland's public transport authority, and their website provides comprehensive information on buses, trains, and ferries in the state. You can access timetables, plan your journey, and find fare information through their website.

4. Tourism and Events Queensland (www.queensland.com): This website is an

excellent resource for tourists and visitors. It offers information on popular destinations, attractions, accommodation options, tours, and events happening throughout Queensland. It can help you plan your travel itinerary and discover hidden gems.

Mobile Apps:

1. TransLink (iOS and Android): The TransLink app provides real-time information on public transportation services in Queensland. You can access bus, train, and ferry timetables, plan your journey, and track the arrival times of public transport vehicles.

2. Queensland Tide Times (iOS and Android): This app provides tide times and tidal predictions for various locations along Queensland's coastline. It's useful for those planning beach activities, boating, or fishing, as it helps you determine the best times for high and low tides.

3. Queensland National Parks (iOS and Android): The Queensland National Parks app provides information on national parks, including maps,

walking tracks, camping sites, and facilities. It also offers alerts and updates on park conditions and closures.

4. Emergency Plus (iOS and Android): The Emergency Plus app provides accurate GPS coordinates to emergency services when you're in need of assistance. It can help you relay your location quickly and accurately during an emergency.

5. QAGOMA (iOS and Android): The Queensland Art Gallery and Gallery of Modern Art (QAGOMA) app is designed for art enthusiasts. It provides information on current exhibitions, events, and programs held at the galleries. It also offers multimedia content and audio guides for a more immersive experience.

These websites and mobile apps can be valuable tools for accessing information, planning your travel, staying safe, and exploring the various attractions and services available in Queensland.

MAPS AND NAVIGATION TOOLS

Maps and navigation tools are essential for navigating and exploring Queensland, Australia. Here are some detailed and short information on popular maps and navigation tools in Queensland:

1. Google Maps (www.google.com/maps):
   Google Maps is a widely used online mapping service available on both desktop and mobile platforms. It offers detailed maps of Queensland, including streets, landmarks, and points of interest. It provides directions for driving, walking, cycling, and public transportation. The app also includes real-time traffic information and can help you find nearby businesses, restaurants, and attractions.

2. Apple Maps (www.apple.com/maps):
   Apple Maps is a mapping application pre-installed on Apple devices. It offers detailed maps of Queensland, including turn-by-turn navigation, traffic information, and public transportation directions. The app integrates well

with other Apple services and devices, making it convenient for users within the Apple ecosystem.

3. Here WeGo (www.here.com):

Here WeGo is a versatile mapping and navigation tool available on various platforms. It provides detailed maps of Queensland and offers turn-by-turn navigation for driving, walking, and public transportation. The app also includes real-time traffic updates and the ability to download offline maps for use without an internet connection.

4. Queensland Roads (www.qldtraffic.qld.gov.au):

The Queensland Roads website provides interactive maps with real-time traffic information. It helps you stay updated on road conditions, incidents, and roadworks in Queensland. The maps show traffic congestion, road closures, and alternative routes, allowing you to plan your journey accordingly.

5. Wikiloc (www.wikiloc.com):

Wikiloc is a community-driven platform that offers a collection of user-generated GPS tracks and trails. It's particularly useful for outdoor enthusiasts and hikers in Queensland. The app provides access to a vast database of trails, including hiking routes, cycling paths, and off-road tracks. Users can upload and download GPS tracks, view trail maps, and read reviews and tips from fellow adventurers.

These maps and navigation tools can assist you in planning your routes, finding points of interest, and navigating Queensland efficiently. Remember to use them responsibly, follow local traffic laws, and prioritise safety while driving or exploring the region.

TRAVELLING WITH CHILDREN AND FAMILY

Travelling with children and family in Queensland can be a wonderful experience. Here are some detailed and short tips to make your family trip enjoyable:

1. Choose Family-Friendly Accommodation:

Look for accommodations that cater to families, such as resorts, hotels with family rooms or suites, or holiday parks with kid-friendly facilities. These accommodations often provide amenities like swimming pools, playgrounds, kids' clubs, and family-friendly dining options.

2. Plan Age-Appropriate Activities:

Consider the interests and ages of your children when planning activities. Queensland offers a wide range of family-friendly attractions, including theme parks like Dreamworld, Sea World, and Warner Bros. Movie World. Other options include wildlife sanctuaries, interactive museums, water parks, and beautiful beaches suitable for kids.

3. Be Sun-Smart:

Queensland's climate can be quite sunny and hot, so it's crucial to protect your children from the sun. Apply sunscreen with a high SPF, encourage them to wear hats, sunglasses, and protective clothing, and seek shade during the hottest parts of the day. Stay hydrated and make sure your kids drink plenty of water.

4. Check Safety Regulations:

If you plan to rent a car or use public transportation, ensure that you have appropriate child car seats or restraints to comply with safety regulations. Familiarise yourself with the laws and guidelines regarding child safety in vehicles. It's also essential to follow safety instructions at attractions and ensure that activities are suitable for your children's age and abilities.

5. Take Breaks and Rest:

Travelling can be tiring for children, so plan regular breaks and allow time for rest and relaxation. Children may need downtime to recharge and adjust to new environments. Consider incorporating activities that allow for breaks, such as picnics in parks or leisurely walks along the beach.

6. Pack Essentials:

Pack essential items such as snacks, water bottles, diapers, wipes, spare clothing, and any necessary medications. Having these items readily available can make your family outings more convenient and comfortable. Also, bring along entertainment options like books, toys, or tablets to keep children occupied during travel or downtime.

7. Stay Connected and Safe:
Ensure that you have emergency contact numbers saved in your phone and keep a copy of important documents, including passports and medical information. Establish a meeting point if you get separated in crowded areas. It's also a good idea to use a location-sharing app or wearable device to keep track of your children's whereabouts.

Remember to be flexible and allow for spontaneity during your family trip. Embrace the opportunities to create lasting memories and enjoy the unique experiences that Queensland has to offer for travellers of all ages.

APPENDIX

SAMPLE ITINERARIES FOR QUEENSLAND

Sure! Here are a few sample itineraries for Queensland, Australia, highlighting some of the best destinations and activities the region has to offer:

1. Tropical Adventure:
    - Day 1-3: Start your journey in Cairns, explore the Great Barrier Reef, and go snorkelling or diving among colourful coral reefs.
    - Day 4-6: Head to Port Douglas and take a scenic drive along the coast to the Daintree Rainforest, where you can go jungle trekking and visit Cape Tribulation.
    - Day 7-9: Fly to the Whitsunday Islands and spend your days sailing, relaxing on white sandy beaches, and exploring the stunning Whitehaven Beach.

- Day 10-12: Wrap up your adventure in Townsville, where you can visit Magnetic Island, hike the trails of Castle Hill, and learn about marine life at the Reef HQ Aquarium.

2. Coastal Escape:
  - Day 1-3: Begin in Brisbane, the vibrant capital of Queensland. Explore the city's cultural attractions, visit the Lone Pine Koala Sanctuary, and enjoy the South Bank Parklands.
  - Day 4-6: Travel north to the Sunshine Coast and spend time in Noosa. Relax on the pristine beaches, explore Noosa National Park, and take a scenic drive to the nearby hinterland towns of Montville and Maleny.
  - Day 7-9: Continue your coastal journey to the Gold Coast. Enjoy the famous surf beaches, visit theme parks like Dreamworld and SeaWorld, and explore the Gold Coast Hinterland with its stunning waterfalls and rainforest walks.
  - Day 10-12: End your trip on the beautiful Fraser Coast. Take a 4x4 tour on Fraser Island, the world's largest sand island, swim in crystal-clear lakes, and spot wildlife like dingoes and whales (during the migration season).

3. Outback and Reef Exploration:

   - Day 1-3: Fly into Cairns and explore the Great Barrier Reef, as mentioned in the first itinerary.

   - Day 4-6: Journey west to the Outback town of Mount Isa. Visit the Outback at Isa museum, explore underground mines, and learn about the region's mining heritage.

   - Day 7-9: Continue your Outback adventure in Longreach. Visit the Australian Stockman's Hall of Fame, take a sunset cruise on the Thomson River, and experience outback life at a cattle station.

   - Day 10-12: Conclude your trip to Airlie Beach and the Whitsunday Islands, enjoying the pristine beaches, sailing opportunities, and relaxing atmosphere.

Remember to adjust the duration and activities based on your preferences and the time available. These itineraries provide a glimpse of the diverse experiences Queensland has to offer, whether you're seeking adventure, coastal beauty, or outback exploration.

PACKING CHECKLIST FOR QUEENSLAND

When packing for Queensland, it's important to consider the region's climate, which is generally warm and tropical. Here's a detailed packing checklist to help you prepare:

1. Clothing:
   - Lightweight and breathable clothing such as t-shirts, shorts, skirts, and dresses.
   - Swimwear for beach and pool activities.
   - Light long-sleeved shirts and pants for sun protection.
   - Comfortable walking shoes or sandals.
   - Hat or cap to shield yourself from the sun.
   - Light rain jacket or umbrella, as tropical showers can occur.

2. Accessories:
   - Sunglasses to protect your eyes from the bright sun.
   - Sunscreen with a high SPF for adequate sun protection.

- Insect repellent to prevent mosquito bites.
- A reusable water bottle to stay hydrated.
- A daypack or beach bag for carrying your essentials.
- Snorkeling gear if you plan to explore the Great Barrier Reef.

3. Electronics and Documents:
   - Travel adapters for charging your devices.
   - Camera or smartphone for capturing memories.
   - Waterproof phone case or pouch for water-based activities.
   - Any necessary travel documents, including your passport, ID, and travel insurance information.
   - A copy of your itinerary and emergency contact numbers.

4. Health and Personal Care:
   - Personal medications and prescriptions.
   - Basic first aid kit with band-aids, antiseptic cream, and any necessary medications.
   - Toiletries including toothbrush, toothpaste, and travel-sized shampoo and conditioner.

- Hand sanitizer for maintaining hygiene on the go.

5. Miscellaneous:
  - Cash and/or credit cards.
  - Travel guidebook or maps for reference.
  - Snacks for the journey or for outdoor activities.
  - Travel locks for securing your belongings.

Remember to pack light and practical, as Queensland's warm climate calls for comfortable and breathable clothing. It's also a good idea to check the weather forecast for your specific travel dates to ensure you're well-prepared.

GLOSSARY OF AUSTRALIAN TERMS

Sure! Here's a glossary of Australian terms to help you understand some commonly used words and phrases:

1. Aussie: Slang term for an Australian person.

2. G'day: A common Australian greeting, short for "Good day."

3. Mate: A term of friendship used to refer to a friend or acquaintance.

4. Sheila: A slang term for a woman or girl.

5. Barbie: Short for "barbecue," a popular outdoor cooking activity in Australia.

6. Thongs: In Australia, thongs refer to flip-flops or sandals worn on the feet.

7. Arvo: Short for "afternoon."

8. Brekkie: An abbreviation for "breakfast."

9. Outback: The remote and rural areas of Australia, typically characterised by a dry and arid landscape.

10. Maccas: Slang term for McDonald's.

11. Bottle-O: Short for "bottle shop," which is a liquor store.

12. BYO: "Bring Your Own." Often used in restaurants to indicate that you can bring your own alcohol.

13. Esky: A portable cooler or ice box used for keeping drinks and food cold.

14. Ute: Short for "utility vehicle," a pickup truck.

15. Bogan: A colloquial term used to describe someone who is perceived as uncultured or unsophisticated.

16. Tinnie: A can of beer, or a small aluminium boat.

17. Servo: Short for "service station," which is a petrol/gas station.

18. Op-shop: Short for "opportunity shop," which is a thrift store or second-hand store.

19. Bikkie: Short for "biscuit," which refers to cookies.

20. Swag: A portable sleeping unit used by campers, typically made of canvas.

These are just a few examples of Australian terms and slang that you might encounter during your visit to Australia. The unique language and expressions add to the country's cultural charm.

CONVERSION TABLES FOR UNITS AND CURRENCY

Certainly! Here are some conversion tables for units and currency commonly used in Queensland, Australia:

1. Units Conversion:

Length:
- 1 kilometre (km) = 0.6214 miles (mi)
- 1 metre (m) = 3.2808 feet (ft)

- 1 centimetre (cm) = 0.3937 inches (in)

Temperature:
- Celsius (°C) to Fahrenheit (°F): Multiply by 9/5 and add 32.
- Fahrenheit (°F) to Celsius (°C): Subtract 32 and multiply by 5/9.

Volume:
- 1 litre (L) = 0.2642 gallons (gal)
- 1 litre (L) = 1.0567 quarts (qt)
- 1 millilitre (mL) = 0.0338 fluid ounces (fl oz)

Weight:
- 1 kilogram (kg) = 2.2046 pounds (lb)
- 1 gram (g) = 0.0353 ounces (oz)
- 1 metric ton (t) = 1,000 kilograms (kg)

2. Currency Conversion:

The currency used in Queensland and Australia is the Australian Dollar (AUD). The exchange rate can vary, so it's best to check the current rates before your trip. Here are some approximate conversions as of the time of writing:

- 1 Australian Dollar (AUD) is approximately 0.75 US Dollar (USD).
- 1 Australian Dollar (AUD) is approximately 0.67 Euro (EUR).
- 1 Australian Dollar (AUD) is approximately 0.58 British Pound (GBP).
- 1 Australian Dollar (AUD) is approximately 82 Japanese Yen (JPY).
- 1 Australian Dollar (AUD) is approximately 1.09 New Zealand Dollar (NZD).

Keep in mind that exchange rates fluctuate, so it's advisable to check the current rates closer to your travel dates. You can do so at currency exchange offices, banks, or through online currency converters.

These conversion tables should help you convert between different units and currencies while in Queensland.

APPRECIATION

Dear valued customers,

We would like to express our heartfelt appreciation for choosing the Queensland Travel Guide 2023 by Silva Martin. Your decision to trust us as your source of information and inspiration for exploring Queensland is truly humbling.

With this travel guide, we have strived to provide you with a comprehensive and insightful resource that captures the essence of this magnificent destination. We understand that planning a trip can be overwhelming, but we hope that our guide will serve as your trusted companion, helping you navigate the wonders of Queensland with ease.

Through meticulous research, detailed descriptions, and stunning visuals, we aimed to showcase the breathtaking landscapes, vibrant cities, and hidden gems that make Queensland a dream destination. From the pristine beaches of the Gold Coast to the ancient rainforests of the

Daintree, our guide offers a glimpse into the diverse and awe-inspiring beauty that awaits you.

Your support in choosing our travel guide encourages us to continue our pursuit of excellence in delivering valuable content. We sincerely hope that our guide enhances your travel experience, enables you to discover new places, and creates unforgettable memories along the way.

We would also like to extend our gratitude for your contribution to the local communities and businesses in Queensland. Your decision to explore this region not only enriches your own life but also supports the preservation of its natural wonders and the livelihoods of its residents.

Once again, thank you for choosing the Queensland Travel Guide 2023 by Silva Martin. We are honoured to be a part of your travel journey and look forward to serving you in the future. Safe travels and may your time in Queensland be filled with joy, adventure, and cherished moments.

Warm regards,

The Silva Martin Team